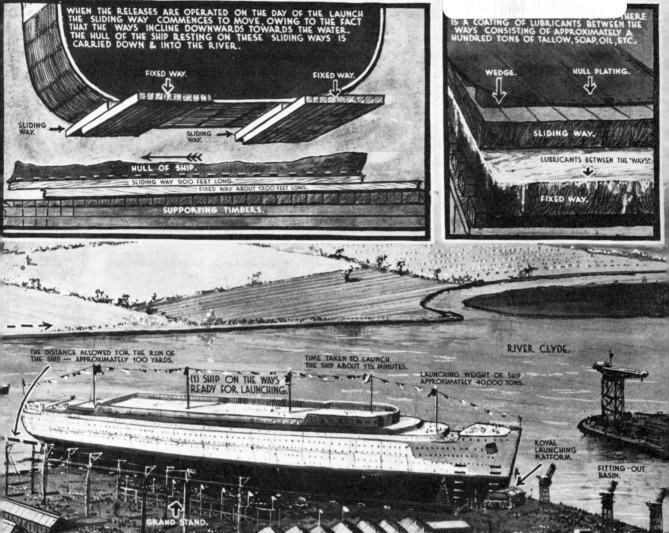

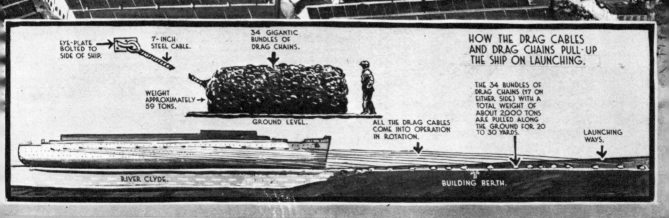

to Sasha,
my son.
R.L.

THE QUEENS OF THE NORTH ATLANTIC

By Robert Lacey

STEIN AND DAY/*Publishers*/New York

CONTENTS

Designed by Ken Carroll

First published in the United States of America, 1976
Copyright © 1973 by Robert Lacey
and Sidgwick & Jackson Limited
All rights reserved
Printed in Great Britain
Stein and Day/*Publishers*/Scarborough House,
Briarcliff Manor, N.Y. 10510

Library of Congress Cataloging in Publication Data
Lacey, Robert.
   The Queens of the North Atlantic
   1. Queen Mary (Steamship)   2. Queen Elizabeth
(Ship)   I. Title.
VM383. Q4L3   1976   387.2'43   75-35915
ISBN 0-8128-1935-7

Opposite and previous page: the launching of *Queen Elizabeth*

E. J. FROST

WEEKLY
ILLUSTRATED

Saturday,
Oct. 1,
1938

2ᴰ

No. 14
Vol. V

THE QUEEN ACCOMPANIED BY PRINCESS
ELIZABETH AND PRINCESS MARGARET
ROSE LAUNCHES THE 'QUEEN ELIZABETH'

LAUNCHING OF THE 'QUEEN ELIZABETH' ★ EXCLUSIVE PICTURES OF THE CRISIS

Picture Credits

Daily Express – pp 4–5.

Radio Times Hulton Picture Library – pp 6, 12 & 13, 21 (all), 22 & 23, 24, 26 & 27, 29 (all), 30 & 31, 34 & 35, 38, 40, 45 (top), 50 (top), 53, 105, 110, 111 (both), 117 (both).

Syndication International – pp 9, 50 (bottom).

The Cunard Steam Ship Co Ltd – pp 15, 46 & 47, 49, 54 & 55 (all), 68 & 69 (all), 70 (both), 78 & 79, 90 (inset).

Illustrated London News – pp 16 & 17, 37.

Mansell Collection – p 19.

Popperfoto – pp 42 & 43.

Ocean Pictures, Southampton – pp 57, 102 & 103 (all), 118 (both).

Conway Picture Library – pp 58 & 59 (all), 106 & 107, 115, 120 & 121.

Central Press – p 60.

Keystone Press – pp 62 & 63, 64 & 65, 82 & 83, 85 (bottom), 109.

Imperial War Museum – pp 85 (top), 88 (both), 90 & 91.

Press Association – pp 94 & 95, 97.

Southern Newspapers Ltd – pp 98 & 99.

United Press International – p 123 (middle).

Long Beach Bureau – p 123 (top).

We are most grateful for the help we have received in the preparation of this book from William Armstrong, Joe Avrach, William Blackmore, Clive Butler, Leslie and Stuart Hunter Cox of Ocean Pictures, Peter Coxson, the Cunard Steam Ship Company, John Frost, Wendy Gow, Douglas Lobley, the London Library, the Long Beach News Bureau, Jamie Maxtone-Graham, R. S. Medus, the Museum of the Sea, Long Beach, California, Philip Norman, Joan Owen, Jaqueline Reynolds, the Steamship Historical Society of America and Hans Tasiemka.

We are grateful to the following for copyright material: Charles Scribner's Sons for an extract from F. Scott Fitzgerald's *The Rough Crossing* (copyright 1929 Curtis Publishing Co.); The Delacorte Press/Seymour Lawrence for an extract from J. M. Brinnin's *The Sway of the Grand Saloon*; Houghton Mifflin Co. for an extract from Winston S. Churchill's *The Second World War*.

PROLOGUE

F. Scott Fitzgerald

Once on the long, covered piers, you have come into a ghostly country that is no longer Here and not yet There. Especially at night. There is a hazy yellow vault full of shouting, echoing voices. There is the rumble of trucks and the clump of trunks, the strident chatter of a crane and the first salt smell of the sea. You hurry through, even though there's time. The past, the continent, is behind you; the future is that glowing mouth in the side of the ship, this dim turbulent alley is too confusedly the present.

Up the gangplank, and the vision of the world adjusts itself, narrows. One is a citizen of a commonwealth smaller than Andorra. One is no longer so sure of anything. Curiously unmoved the men at the purser's desk, cell-like the cabin, disdainful the eyes of voyagers and their friends, solemn the officer who stands on the deserted promenade deck thinking something of his own as he stares at the crowd below. A last odd idea that one didn't really have to come, then the loud mournful whistles, and the thing – certainly not the boat, but rather a human idea, a frame of mind – pushes forth into the big dark night.

(The Rough Crossing)

1. THE AGE OF THE ATLANTIC PALACES

From the generation
before the Queens: the *Lusitania*
– sunk by a U-boat in 1915

It began with a fraud. In 1819 the steamship *Savannah* claimed the first mechanically powered crossing of the North Atlantic, steaming out of Savannah and into Liverpool with her smoke stack belching proudly. But in the twenty-six days in between she had relied on her sails and had only raised steam six times.

Isambard Kingdom Brunel, however, was intrigued by the deceit. The *Savannah* had been built like a sailing ship, with fuel space for only eighty hours steaming out of 663. But Brunel calculated that while the usable hull space was increased by the cube of a ship's length, its resistance in the water – and the driving power demanded of its engines – was only squared. Thus was born one of the great maxims that was to shape the vessels of the North Atlantic run – the bigger the better: the longer the ship the larger the fuel capacity, the bigger the engines and the more spacious the passenger accommodation. From the *Savannah* and Brunel's simple equation sprang grand saloons and swimming pools, state-rooms and shopping arcades, the maritime metropoli that were to reach their zenith in the thousand-foot-long Cunarder Queens.

Brunel's *Great Western* was but a cottage compared to those great floating castles, but her saloon was seventy-one feet by twenty-one just the same, and was the wonder of Bristol as the ship was floated out into the brown Avon there on 19 July 1837. The saloon compared favourably, pronounced one visitor, with those 'of the clubhouses of London in luxury and magnificence; the painted panels of its walls depicting rural scenery, agriculture, music, and arts and sciences, interior views and landscapes, and parties grouped, or engaged in elegant sports and amusements.' Smaller panels 'contained beautifully pencilled paintings of Cupid, Psyche, and other aerial figures.'

And thus was born another great tradition of North Atlantic travel, the necessity for the essentially functional nature of the means of transport – the ship – to be concealed to the utmost degree possible in a forest of baroque detail – nymphs, cherubs, shepherdesses, harps, viols – anything, provided it bore not the slightest resemblance to matters nautical. The public rooms of the *Great Western* were not intended to remind their occupants of tar and ropes and flying salt spray but of 'the glorious saloons of France while yet under the luxurious rule of Louis the Fourteenth'. Passengers should forget about the dark and disturbing mysteries of the deep in 'a bower of bliss, a perfect garden of Armidia', relaxing on sofas 'wadded in a most luxuriant style of elegance never hitherto attempted and only dreamed of in the descriptions of the Arabian Nights and the tales of faëry.'

This somewhat worried style of romance was, in fact, to be eschewed by Samuel Cunard. His sober-sided ships, embellished wherever the profit-motive allowed with anchors and dolphins rather than with satyrs and pipes of Pan, were to be triumphs of realistic marine engineering over pleasure garden fantasies. Where imagination did escape in the gangways of his lean liners it was to express itself in mermaids and tritons that at least acknowledged the perpetual motion that the land-based decorative themes of other vessels attempted to ignore.

But though the two great Cunarder Queens of the twentieth century were to be defiantly sea-going in an era of Odeon gee-gaws and knick-knacks, they were also, above all else, to be *comfortable* – and this can be traced back at least a hundred years to Brunel's *Great Western* of 1837. Though one might imagine that the *Civil Engineer and Architect's Journal* had more important technical innovations to expound to its readers in 1837, it devoted not a little space to the fashion in

Samuel Cunard, founder of the Cunard Line. Born in 1789, the son of a carpenter in Halifax, Nova Scotia, he set the profit-oriented style by which the Queens were to live – and die. Following pages: from the *Illustrated London News*

which the great bridge builder and railway engineer had made it possible for passengers to summon servants to their presence without moving from their beds:

> When the attendance of a steward is required, the passenger pulls the bell-rope in his berth, which rings the bell in the small box (in the stewards' room) and at the same time by means of a small lever forces up through a slit in the lid a small tin label with the number of the room painted requiring the services of the steward, and there remains, until the steward has ascertained the number of the room and pushed it down again. Thus, instead of an interminable number of bells, there are only two. This arrangement, which is alike ingenious as it is useful, is deserving the notice of architects.

From such details was a century of the North Atlantic's social history composed – though theory and practice did not always coincide, for a passenger torn in the worst miseries that the open ocean could inflict gained more solace from an

CUNARDERS OF OTHER DAYS: EPOCH-MAKING
FROM THE PIONEER "BRITANNIA" OF 1840

ILLUSTRATIONS (EXCEPT THOSE OF THE "IVERNIA," "CARMANIA," AND "LUSITANIA") REPRODUCED

1840: THE TYPE OF THE FIRST CUNARDER (1154 TONS)—A DRAWING ENTITLED "CUNARD ROYAL MAIL PADDLE STEAM SHIPS 'BRITANNIA,' 'ACADIA,' 'CALEDONIA,' AND 'COLUMBIA.'"

1848: TWO OF THE FOUR NEW CUNARDERS THEN PLACED ON THE ATLANTIC SERVICE: THE CUNARD ROYAL MAIL PADDLE STEAM SHIPS "EUROPA" AND "AMERICA."

1856: THE 3300-TON CUNARDER "PERSIA," BUILT AS A PADDLE-STEAMER (THOUGH AFTER THE ADOPTION OF SCREW-PROPELLERS) IN DEFERENCE TO THE CONSERVATISM OF PASSENGERS.

1867: ONE OF THE EARLY SCREW-PROPELLED CUNARDERS—THE 2960-TON "RUSSIA," ADMIRED BY NAUTICAL MEN FOR HER "BEAUTY OF OUTLINE AND SYMMETRY OF PROPORTIONS."

1881: THE CUNARD ROYAL MAIL STEEL SCREW STEAM SHIP "SERVIA" (7392 TONS), A "MONSTER VESSEL" OF HER DAY, SECOND ONLY IN SIZE TO THE "GREAT EASTERN."

1883: A LINER THAT CARRIED 480 CABIN PASSENGERS AND 700 STEERAGE: THE 7269-TON "AURANIA," BUILT WITH INCREASED BEAM IN ORDER TO SECURE GREATER STABILITY.

THE CUNARDER THAT SANK THE GERMAN "CAP TRAFALGAR" ON SEPTEMBER 14, 1914: THE 20,000-TON "CARMANIA," COMPLETED IN 1905, AND USED IN THE WAR AS AN ARMED MERCHANT SHIP.

THE immense new Cunard White Star liner, on which public interest has been centred from the time of her inception, and especially since the announcement that the Queen would launch and name her on September 26, represents high-water mark of British shipbuilding. In the illustrations given here (as those on page 467 of this number), it is interesting to trace some of the most important stages in the development of Cunarders since the foundation of famous line. We abridge here some relevant passages in the "History of Cunard Steamship Company," from which most of our illustrations are drawn: "The first four steamships provided by the Company were the 'Britannia,' 'Acadia,' 'Caledonia,' and 'Columbia,' all wooden paddle-wheel vessels built the Clyde in 1840. The 'Britannia,' the pioneer of the fleet, measured 20 long, with a tonnage of 1154, and accommodation for 115 cabin passengers, no steerage. She sailed on her maiden voyage from Liverpool on July 4, 1840. Four new ships, the 'America,' 'Niagara,' 'Canada,' and 'Europa,' took station in the early trade in 1848, being followed in 1850 by the 'Asia' 'Africa,' and in 1852 by the 'Arabia.'" The "Europa" and "Arabia" were am

PREDECESSORS OF THE NEW GIANT LINER; TO THE "LUSITANIA" OF TRAGIC MEMORY.

FROM "THE HISTORY OF THE CUNARD STEAMSHIP COMPANY," BY COURTESY, OF CUNARD WHITE STAR, LTD.

1850 : THE CUNARD ROYAL MAIL PADDLE STEAM SHIP "ASIA"—ONE OF TWO NEW CUNARDERS INTRODUCED INTO THE SERVICE IN THAT YEAR, THE OTHER BEING THE "AFRICA."

1852 : AN ATLANTIC LINER THAT TOOK ITS STATION IN THE TRADE IN THAT YEAR— THE CUNARD ROYAL MAIL PADDLE STEAM SHIP "ARABIA."

ANOTHER TYPE BUILT SOON AFTER THE DISCONTINUANCE OF PADDLE WHEELS : A DRAWING ENTITLED "CUNARD ROYAL MAIL SCREW STEAM SHIPS 'BOTHNIA' AND 'SCYTHIA.'"

1872-8 : THE CUNARD ROYAL MAIL SCREW STEAM SHIP "GALLIA" (OF 4809 TONS), THE LAST OF SEVEN SHIPS ADDED TO THE CUNARD FLEET DURING THAT PERIOD.

1884-5 : A TYPE THAT MARKED A GREAT ADVANCE IN THE EVOLUTION OF PASSENGER LINERS—A DRAWING ENTITLED "CUNARD ROYAL MAIL STEEL SCREW STEAM SHIPS 'UMBRIA' AND 'ETRURIA.'"

ONE OF THE CUNARD WAR CASUALTIES : THE "IVERNIA," SUNK BY A SUBMARINE IN THE MEDITERRANEAN ON JANUARY 1, 1917, WHILE EMPLOYED AS A TRANSPORT, WITH THE LOSS OF ABOUT 150 LIVES.

THE VICTIM OF AN "APPALLING CRIME" : THE GREAT CUNARDER "LUSITANIA" (30,396 TONS), TORPEDOED BY A GERMAN SUBMARINE ON MAY 7, 1915, WITH A LOSS OF NEARLY 1500 LIVES.

several Cunarders employed in the Crimean War of 1854.——In 1856, "notwithstanding that the screw propeller had proved advantageous, passengers were as yet unwilling to take leave of the old paddle-wheel, rapidly becoming extinct. The Company decided to defer to the feelings of their passengers, and the 'Persia' was built. Another vessel of the same class, the 'Scotia,' was the last of the paddle-wheels.——The 'Russia,' built on the Clyde in 1867, was tastefully furnished for 235 cabin passengers. Her fastest passage was 8 days 28 minutes. ——In the six years (from 1872) the Company increased their fleet by seven large screw steamers (fitted with compound engines), of which the last was the 'Gallia' (4809 tons)." ——A "monster" vessel, named "Servia," completed in 1881, was the largest and most powerful ship, except the "Great Eastern," up to that time constructed. Her length was 515 ft. and gross tonnage 7392.——The "Aurania," a fresh type of 1883, had increased beam to secure greater stability and a more commodious saloon.—The "Umbria" (1884) and "Etruria" (1885) were in their day "the greatest triumphs of modern shipbuilding science." Their length was 501 ft. and gross tonnage 7718. The "Etruria's" fastest passage, from Queenstown to New York, was 6 days, 6 hours, 36 minutes.——The sinking of the "Ivernia," while used as a transport in the war, was illustrated in our issue of Feb. 3, 1917.

agonized bellow than from a bell-rope – as was discovered on the *Great Western*'s maiden voyage:

> Sea sickness stalks in stifling horror among us and the dreadful cry of 'Steward! Steward!' – the last ejaculation of despair – comes from a dozen nooks, hurried in a piercing treble or growled forth with muttered maledictions on the dilatory bucket bearer or in the deep tones of thorough bass.

Still, the *Great Western*'s passengers had to suffer for an unprecedentedly short time – fourteen and a half days, a bare fortnight. Well might the Bristol *Mirror* compare 'the joy and pleasure announced by all classes . . . in the city' with 'the tidings from the Nile, Trafalgar Bay and the plains of Waterloo'. As Britain and America celebrated the dawn of a new era – with only muted doubts as to whether they really *wanted* to be this close – only a businessman in Halifax, Nova Scotia, ventured some reservation about the prevailing steam-ship fever:

> 'We have received your letter of the twenty second instant,' wrote Samuel Cunard to Messrs. Ross and Primrose of Pictou, who had invited him in 1829 to lend his ship-owning expertise to their plans to start up a steamship line. 'We are entirely unacquainted with the cost of a steamboat, and would not like to embark in a business of which we are quite ignorant. Must, therefore decline taking part in the one you propose getting up.'

Samuel Cunard had made his money by cautious investment in merchant sailing ships. There was no point in him now moving into steam transport unless he was sure that his own risk capital would be absolutely safe – which was why he waited on the announcement that the British government was willing to subsidize a steam service to carry the mails between London and Halifax (and thence to New York) before he committed himself definitely to the new style of maritime propulsion. He came to England – as a resident of Canada he was a British subject the equal of any home-based shipping magnate – and, largely on the strength of his record with sailing ships, was able to persuade the Lords of the Admiralty that he could supply the mail service they needed for just £55,000 a year.

The postal contract was to prove the foundation of the Cunard fortunes. When the two Queens came to be sketched out in the 1920s it was primarily as mail packets that they were designed, since carrying the royal mail provided a guaranteed subsidy for innovation and a cushion against adversity – and it was Samuel Cunard's shrewd eye which first spotted this and took advantage of it. His hard-headedness was underlined by the order he placed with Robert Napier, the Clydeside ship-builder, once he had been awarded his contract:

> I shall require one or two steamboats of 300 horsepower and about 800 tons. I shall want these vessels to be of the very best description, plain and comfortable, not the least unnecessary expense for show. I prefer plain woodwork in the cabin, and it will save a large amount in the cost.

'Plain woodwork in the cabin.' Robert Napier did not like that. But Samuel Cunard knew the style in which he intended to make the North Atlantic his own: not Gothic or Baroque or Pastoral but just plain profitable. And in that same tradition a century later the great Queens were to be built – and scrapped the moment they ceased to make money. The *Britannia*, sailing on her maiden voyage on 4 July 1840, the first of the Cunard steamship fleet, was not the most elegant or ostentatious vessel plying the North Atlantic, but she was the most functional. Running into Halifax she logged on Thursday 16 July 1840, 278 nautical miles – a greater distance than any other steamship had yet covered in twenty-four hours.

And plain though her cabin woodwork might be, she looked after her passengers with a thoroughness that was to become another Cunard tradition. The wines and spirits bar opened every morning at 6 a.m. – steak with a bottle of hock seems to have been a popular breakfast – and while passengers enjoyed this morning collation their bedroom stewards were lining up on the leeward side of the ship to empty the chamber pots that had been charged during the night.

In the early 1840s the *Britannia*, along with her sister ships the *Caledonia*, *Acadia*, and *Columbia*, established for the Cunard line, already identified by its lurid orange-red, and black smoke-stack stripings, a solid reputation with passengers for speed and comfort, while the guaranteed subsidy provided by the mail packet contract under-pinned the whole enterprise. When the disappearance of the *President*, a rival liner over thirty feet longer than the *Great Western*, scared passengers away in the 1840s – ' I cannot help wondering what we would do if the Monster exploded in mid-Ocean' – the contract with the Admiralty kept the four Cunard vessels solvent and steaming with unflappable regularity.

Other challengers came and went through the nineteenth century, foundering in difficulties which Cunard's plain efficiency, realism and guaranteed income from the British Government sailed smoothly over. There was Edward Knight Collins who, with the help of the *American* mail contract, determined 'to proceed with the absolute conquest of this man Cunard' by fitting out a plush fleet with all the fripperies of Mississippi riverboats – forty tons of ice in the kitchen, a

Below: the baroque luxury of the floating palaces; a typical 19th-century saloon in which you could be anywhere but at sea

barber's shop and a smoking room. The feasts with which he regaled his passengers made the Cunard menu look like the efforts of a workhouse on a tight budget:

Soups – Green turtle, Potage au choux
Boiled – Hams, Tongues, Cold corned beef, Turkeys (oyster sauce), Fowl (parsley sauce), Leg of mutton (caper sauce)
Fish – Cod (stuffed and baked), Boiled bass (Hollander sauce)
Roast – Beef, Veal, Mutton, Lamb, Geese (champagne sauce), Ducks, Pigs, Turkey, Fowls
Entrées – Macaroni au gratin, Filet of pigeon au Cronstaugh, Croquette de poisson à la Richelieu, Salmi de canard sauvage, Poulets (pique, sauce tomato), Cotelette de veau à la St Gara, Fricandeau de tortue au petit pois, d'Oyeis en cassis, Epigram d'agneau (sauce truppe)
Vegetables – Green corn, Green peas
Salads – Potato and plain
Pastry – Baked vermicelli pudding, Apple fritters (hard sauce), Almond cup custards, Red currant tartlets, Apple tarts, Open puffs, Cranberry tarts, Coventry puffs, etc.
Desserts – Fruit, Nuts, Olives, Cakes, etc. etc. Coffee, Lemonade (frozen)

But the Collins fortune melted like the ice round the exotic fruit and game which wrecked his budgets – while his ships shook themselves to pieces for speed records that proved pointless when achieved at the cost of passengers' safety. Cunarders could not boast exotic cuisines, but they had never lost a single life.

The White Star Line made much stiffer competition for canny Samuel – dubbed Sir Samuel by Queen Victoria on Lord Palmerston's recommendation after Cunard ships had been taken off the North Atlantic in the 1850s to ferry the Light Brigade and thousands of other hapless British soldiers to their deaths in the Crimea. In 1870 White Star launched the *Oceanic* with electric bells that summoned stewards 'with the touch of the finger to the ivory disc', taps instead of water jugs, oil lamps instead of candles, bathtubs, and central heating, and, an improvement even on E. K. Collins's barber's shop, hairbrushes that brushed mechanically! It was all the work, explained White Star's brochure, of that Victorian hero – steam: 'Like the elephant that picks up a needle and [also] tears down a tree, there is no task too small, no work too great for the giant, steam. He warms the child's berth; he weighs the anchor. He turns the barber's brush. He loads and discharges the ship; and rests not night nor day.'

Passengers seemed for a while almost to believe that He worked for White Star alone. The '-ias' of Cunard (*Britannia, Acadia, Caledonia, Columbia, Persia*) were deserted in favour of the '-ics' of White Star (*Oceanic, Baltic, Repulsic, Adriatic, Celtic*). But from that same line came the *Atlantic* which, in April 1873, went down off Nova Scotia with the loss of some 500 souls, the worst transatlantic disaster in history until the most famous of all the White Star '-ics', the *Titanic*, also sank one clear starry night some forty years later.

Meanwhile Cunard retained its remarkable safety record, mainly because of the care with which the company trained its crews and captains – as Mark Twain testified:

The Cunard people would not take Noah himself as first mate till they had worked him up through all the lower grades and tried him ten years on such matter. They make every officer serve an apprenticeship under their eyes in their own ships before

Top: the Cunarder *Mauretania*, holder of the Blue Riband for 22 years. Centre: lounge of the *Lusitania*. Some of the early interiors looked like grand hotels, others like gentlemen's clubs. Bottom: promenade deck on the *Lusitania*, the most tragic Cunarder

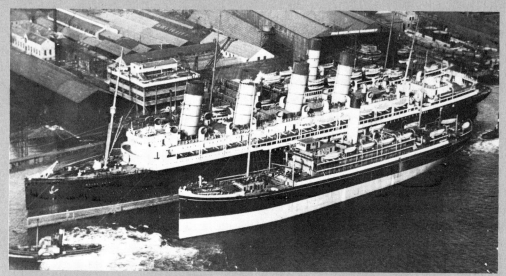

Previous pages: palm court of the *Majestic*, flagship of the White Star Line, Cunard's principal British competitor. Above: Hampshire County Ball held on board the *Majestic*. Originally the German liner, *Bismarck*, she came to White Star in 1922 as a spoil of war

they advance him or trust him. It takes them about ten or fifteen years to manufacture a captain, but when they have got him manufactured to suit at last, they have full confidence in him. The only order they give a captain is this, brief and to the point: 'Your ship is loaded, take her; speed is nothing; follow your own road, deliver her safe, bring her back safe – safety is all that is required.'

Safety first and, after the death of Sir Samuel in 1865, even a little luxury as well. The company went public and, carefully retaining the financial priorities of its late founder, produced a series of vessels, the *Servia*, the *Aurania*, *Umbria* and *Etruria*, which proved that the safest liner fleet on the North Atlantic could more than adequately provide its passengers with creature comforts. The *Servia* boasted the first incandescent electric lamps, the *Umbria* the first refrigerating machinery, while the *Etruria* sported thirteen marble bathrooms with steam and shower apparatus. In the 1890s were launched the *Campania* and the *Lucania*, well upholstered, carpeted and veneered palaces where geraniums bloomed in the ladies' rooms while, at the same time as catering for the luxury end of the market, Cunard provided do-it-yourself budget trips for a less affluent clientele – emigrants drawn to a future in the New World or young American students attracted by the past in the Old. With a bicycle and a hundred dollars an American lad bound for the Ponte Vecchio could, promised a Boston travel agent, look forward to a summer of 'pure, unadulterated fun'.

Go first and buy a bottle or two of coffee essence, some lump sugar and a couple of cans of condensed milk. Get a couple of bottles of pickles. Bring your own towels and a cake of soap. Bring a pillow, then get a camp stool or a cheap steamer's chair. It will not cost much and you can leave it at Southampton till you return. Sitting accommodation is always bad and hard to be got going steerage.

When you get your ticket stamped in the office at the head of the wharf and are at last on deck, scuttle down into the steerage hold, and throw your satchel into the vacant top bunk, as near the middle of the vessel as possible, and stay by it until the bunks are all taken up. You will find a clean colored blanket in your bunk and a straw mattress. There will probably be twenty bunks in your compartment, and you will find that the stewards have put all English speaking people together. They will all be single men where you are; married couples and children in the other side, and further from you, where you will not be allowed to go, the single women.

You will find in your bunk a large black tin cup, a deep soup plate, with 'Cunard Line' stamped on its white surface, a knife, fork and large spoon, all of which you are expected to keep clean yourself. This will be your bill of fare: Beef soup or pea soup, with a scrap or two of meat in your plate, a tin of coffee, and plenty of very good bread and butter, breakfast, at eight o'clock; at eleven, your tin full of nice beef soup, plenty of beef, very good, but nearly always fresh, and potatoes; at supper, five o'clock, bread, butter and tea. On Friday you will have soup in the morning, but no meat, and fish at dinner; you will have pudding at Sunday's dinner, and a little marmalade once or twice in the evening. You will find every thing scrupulously neat on board, and try to help that thing by keeping your bunk and your dishes neat. Keep a watch, too, on fellows who will try to steal your clean dishes and leave their dirty ones in place of yours; that is about the only kind of stealing you need fear.

There is, of course, a deal of quiet flirtation going on, some of the prettiest girls finding it not difficult to pick up admirers even among the first and second class passengers, who occasionally come to the steerage deck. In this amusement the lines of nationality are not drawn. The crew, on the whole, are jolly good fellows, willing to oblige and be obliged, being always ready to take a quarter out of you if they can.

At nine o'clock all women go below, very reluctantly. Then, if you are a wise man, is the time to take your exercise. The air is deliciously cool, there is no crowd, and a calm moonlight or starlight night at sea, if you are alone with a companion who has sense enough to keep silent, is beautiful. If you are an imaginative man, the vastness of this great earth then first dawns upon you, when you see yourself rushing day after day with such speed over it, and yet know how little of its mighty circle you have turned.

The twentieth century was bringing new ways to Cunard and the North Atlantic – package holidays, and ferocious competition that was to culminate in the two ultimate ships, the *Queen Mary* and the *Queen Elizabeth*. Driven by the bitter nationalism that was brewing for the First World War, the German liner fleets of Hamburg-Amerika and Norddeutsche Lloyd, efficient, regular and reliable enterprises since the 1850s, now began to set the pace on the North Atlantic with new style. In 1897, the very year in which Queen Victoria's jubilee was intended to celebrate the triumph of all things British, the significantly named *Kaiser Wilhelm der Grosse*, with space for the unprecedented number of 2,300 passengers, plunged into the water to cross the Atlantic at twenty-one knots and snatch at her very first attempt the Blue Riband, that non-existent but ever more fiercely contested garland worn round the funnels of the most speedy liner between America and England. Not only did the *Kaiser Wilhelm* keep up her remarkable speed for the extra distance between England and Germany, but she was also gilded with extravagant Wagnerian ornaments – and could boast in addition a fine German band. This was a noted feature of all Teutonic liners:

It is pleasant to be summoned to one's meals not by a barbarous gong but by a civilized and inspiring bugle. Only musicians are employed as second-class stewards, and an excellent band plays on deck every morning, so that even sea-sick passengers are reheartened. Who of us will ever forget the sweet, deep pleasure of being awakened on Sunday morning by the playing of 'Nearer, My God, to Thee?'

Nor did the great Valkyries launched at the instigation of Kaiser Wilhelm represent the only, or even principal, threat to the Cunard standard. Junius Pierpoint Morgan, an American to match the Mellons, Rockefellers and Carnegies in his ability to acquire and brandish wealth in defiance of the rules of chance, justice or, on occasions, morality, conceived a plan to monopolize the North Atlantic. He would gain control of every single steamer line and would regiment all the leviathans into a regular ferry service departing like trains from New York once or twice a day at fixed rates, from which his own company, International Mercantile Marine, would take its profit. When in 1902 he added the great White Star Line to the clutch of smaller lines he owned, and also concluded a mutual agreement with Hamburg-Amerika and Norddeutsche Lloyd, Cunard was suddenly and menacingly isolated as the single substantial rival to the largest passenger steamship combine the world had ever seen.

Cunard's reaction was worthy of wily old Sir Samuel himself. Government money had always provided the under-pinning of the company's fortunes and now, cashing in shamelessly on the hysteria of pre-war jingoism by appearing to capitulate to the American multi-millionaire, Cunard extracted from the British Treasury a vast loan of £2,600,000 at only 2¾ per cent interest, with an annual subsidy of £150,000 into the bargain. Britain's standard bearer on the North Atlantic was saved to redeem her country's honour – and to make more money than ever for her shareholders. A brand new generation of Cunarder liners was born, the *Caronia* and *Carmania*, 'the pretty sisters', the *Lusitania*, as long as the Houses of Parliament and taller than the highest building in Northumberland Avenue, and the *Mauretania* which, in 1909, won back the Blue Riband and retained that trophy tightly for no less than twenty-two years.

It was a brilliant triumph for Cunard – not least because the four-funnelled *Mauretania* coupled with her unparalleled speed a strange ability to inspire affection in all who travelled in her. Theodore Dreiser tried to put it into words:

There were several things about this great ship that were unique. It was a beautiful thing all told – its long cherry-wood panelled halls . . . its heavy porcelain baths, its dainty state-rooms fitted with lamps, bureaus, writing-desks, wash-stands, closets and the like. I liked the idea of dressing for dinner and seeing everything quite stately and formal. The little be-buttoned call-boys in their tight-fitting blue suits amused me. And the bugler who bugled for dinner! That was a most musical sound he made, trilling the various quarters gaily as much as to say, 'This is a very joyous event, ladies and gentlemen: we are all happy; come, come; it is a delightful feast.'

Even Franklin Delano Roosevelt, who frankly confessed he disliked travelling in the *Mauretania* – or any ship – had to acknowledge himself captivated by her

Previous pages: the building of the *Aquitania* – launched on the eve of the First World War. Top: dancing on the promenade deck of the *Aquitania* approaching Southampton, 1922. Centre and bottom: swimming pool and ball on *Berengaria*, formerly the German liner *Imperator*. Following pages: orphan children being shown over the *Aquitania* in May 1921

graceful, yachtlike lines, her four enormous black-topped red funnels, and her appearance of power and good breeding:

> Why? Heaven knows! Yet, not for one minute did I ever fail to realize that if there ever was a ship which possessed the thing called 'soul' the *Mauretania* did . . .
>
> Every ship has a soul. But the *Mauretania* had one you could talk to. At times she could be wayward and contrary as a thoroughbred. To no other ship belonged that trick of hers – that thrust and dip and drive into the seas and through them, which would wreck the rails of the Monkey Island with solid sea, or playfully spatter salt water on the Captain's boiled shirt as he took a turn on the bridge before going down to dinner. At other times, she would do everything her Master wanted her to, with a right good will. As Captain Rostron once said to me, she had the manners and deportment of a great lady and behaved herself as such.

Sweeping across the Atlantic to arrive almost always within ten minutes of her scheduled timetable, the *Mauretania* established a sway over the ocean which the sinking of the rival *Titanic* in April 1912 only served to reinforce. And just as the First World War broke out the *Mauretania* was joined by another Cunard ship that had a peculiarly warm and inviting personality of her own, the *Aquitania* – a veritable riot of historical pageantry in which the sober decorative precepts of Sir Samuel were extravagantly ignored:

> As regard the decorations, [said a shipbuilder's journal] a faint echo only of Tudor times and the days of Hans Holbein will be found in some of the decorative details of the *Aquitania*. From this we pass to the days of Sir 'Anthonie' van Dyck and Inigo Jones. But the period of domestic architecture and decorations most completely illustrated in the ship are those which lie between the Restoration of Charles II and the middle of the reign of George III. From the stern classic style of Inigo Jones, Christopher Wren, and the French masters who flourished in the early part of the reign of Louis the Magnificent, we pass gradually to the lighter motives of the Adams and Dances. Full justice is done to the Dutch influences which made themselves strongly felt towards the end of the seventeenth century.

It was a last flamboyant fling before the sad and serious business of war. The 'pretty sister' *Carmania* was armoured and, patrolling the South Atlantic, attacked and sank the *Cap Trafalgar*, the pride of Hamburg-Amerika's South American run, also decked out with guns for the hostilities – the first and last example of a Cunard liner physically doing battle. Then the *Lusitania*, attempting to continue normal passenger services, was tragically caught, on 7 May 1915, in the periscope of U-boat Commander Walther Schwieger off the southern Irish Coast in sight of the Old Head of Kinsale. 'To all of us in the company,' said Cunard, 'the moment we first learned of our loss will remain the most awful moment of our lives – the moment when God Himself seemed to forsake us.' Cunard had lost a life – though the company felt sufficiently absolved from blame to disclaim any financial responsibility to the hundreds bereaved by the catastrophe. A standard reply went out to all claims for compensation:

> Whilst deeply sympathizing with you in your bereavement, we regret that compensation is not payable by the Company under the circumstances, and we can only suggest, therefore, that you communicate with the Under Secretary of State for Foreign Affairs, London, with a view to receiving compensation from Germany at the termination of hostilities.

In the event it was Cunard themselves who got the most handsome compensation when the First World War ended – the great German liner the *Imperator* which, rechristened the *Berengaria*, became with the *Mauretania* and *Aquitania* one of the 'Big Three' of the Cunard fleet refurbished for the excitement of the Aspirin Age. The *Mauretania*, explained a Cunard publicist:

attracts the 'Younger Set' because her clientele are very gay, always, very chic; her sailings are gala nights, with the Junior league at its most junior visible all over the lot ... You will find her decks populous with young girls and young men who more nearly than any other flesh and blood young girls and young men look like the drawings in *Vanity Fair* and *Vogue*. Girls 'just out', sophomores on vacation, whole families of sons and daughters going abroad for the summer or for school. People you've seen on the beach at Southampton or Newport ... on the trails at Hot Springs ... or at the polo at Meadowbrook in the fall. Dancing at dinner in the restaurant, the floor looks like the Ambassador Grill during Christmas vacation. Tea in the lounge, like a coming out party at the Colony Club ...

Twenty years old and ageing fast the *Mauretania* might be, but, claimed the Cunard copywriter, she 'holds the passionate allegiance of whole families of America's highest type, who would rather miss Ascot, or the first day of grouse-shooting than cross in any other ship afloat, but the *Mauretania*.'

The *Berengaria*, the re-christened Teutonic maiden, attracted the ostentatious:

The *Berengaria* is accustomed to move through the night brighter than the Milky Way with the clustered constellations aboard her ... The Queens who cross in the *Berengaria* are the more conspicuous Queens .. the more debonair Mayors choose her. A *Berengaria* sailing is tempestuous with the exploding of flashlights, the pursuit of reporters ... Everything about the *Berengaria* is on the grand, the opulent, scale. She is sensational. Sensational people board her ... Her passenger lists are electric with great names. Great enterprises of finance, of the world worldly, are flung back and forth across her tables ...

The *Aquitania* was, in comparison, the most sober of the 'Big Three', attracting in consequence a more refined type of customer:

The *Aquitania*'s passenger lists tend slightly towards Burke and Debrett. The country family sort of atmosphere ... predisposes in her favor people of social consequence, people of title, people who like their transatlantic crossings to taste of that rather formal sub-division into hierarchies – social, political, hereditary – which mark their lives ... If a ship may be like a house, the *Aquitania* is like some Georgian house of weathered brick that looks through the mist toward the fairy tale outlines of Windsor Castle. A house quiet and beautiful with age without, and inside as modern, as perfectly appointed, as some tower apartment on Park Avenue that has sprung up overnight to forty stories ... The people who cross in her are people you might meet at an important Thursday to Monday, where blood and achievement both count. ... By day, Harris tweeds ... Chanel jerseys ... indolent conversation and energetic sport. By night a sudden increase of tempo ... a blaze of jewels ... the gleam of ivory shoulders ... gowns, rose, gold, green ... Men and women both wearing formality, brilliance, with the perfect ease that is the distinction and delight of aristocratic English life. The same sharp contrast of the extremes of informality and ceremony that makes English country life so stimulating is part of the charm of life, day by day, night by night ...

They were the epitomes of an age and style, the three great liners that ruled the ocean for Cunard in the 1920s. But by the end of that decade they were nearly a quarter of a century out of date and new liners – the *Bremen* and *Europa* for Germany and the *Île de France* – were setting a fresh pace and style on the North Atlantic. It was time for a new great British ship to be created – two, in fact.

2. THE INEVITABLE SHIP

1935: the largest propeller in the world
(35 tons) leaves Millwall for the *Queen Mary*.
The propellers created so much vibration
they had to be scrapped within a year of
the maiden voyage

The WORLD'S LARGEST PROPELLER

WEIGHT, 35, TONS.

MANUFACTURED BY THE

ANGANESE BRONZE & BRASS Cᵒ Lᵀᴰ

FOR THE

S.T.S. QUEEN MARY.

Samuel Cunard's *Britannia* had been a 207-feet-long paddle steamer, capable of keeping up an average speed of eight knots, and ever since 1840 the liners of the North Atlantic had been getting larger and faster. At 790 feet the *Mauretania* could average 26 knots, while the *Aquitania*, scarcely less rapid, was over 900 feet long. But for all the luxury and speed that the ever-extending liners could boast, no shipping company had managed by the mid-1920s to achieve a regular year-round weekly service between Europe and the U.S.A. Though the *Mauretania* could steam from Cherbourg to Ambrose Light in less than five days, and though the *Aquitania* and *Berengaria* worked in harness with her, the three ships could not economically maintain their express service in all weathers. They were, after all, old ladies by the time the twenties were roaring properly, relying on decorous rest and refitting periods to be kept in trim for their transoceanic jaunts.

And so it was that when, in 1926, the directors of the Cunard Steam Ship Company met in their Liverpool headquarters to consider the question of replacements for their Big Three standard bearers, discussion centred on the possibility of establishing a regular weekly shuttle service across the Atlantic, carrying both passengers and mail with a rapidity and precision never seen before. And since, given the ship-building, maintenance and running costs then prevailing, two ships were obviously cheaper than three, the great Queens of the North Atlantic were born, conceived from the first as a pair. They were to be bigger and faster than any other liners in existence – not for the sake of size and speed in themselves but because nothing less could provide the regular weekly service required – as Sir Percy Bates, the chairman of the company, explained:

> The speed is dictated by the time necessary to perform the journey at all seasons of the year, and in both directions, plus the consideration of the number of hours required in port on each side of the Atlantic.
> The size is dictated by the necessity to make money by providing sufficient saleable passenger accommodation to pay for the speed.
> In the opinion of its technical advisers, so far from attempting to construct steamers simply to compete with others in speed and size, the Cunard company is projecting a pair of steamers which, though they will be very large and fast, are, in fact, the smallest and slowest which can fulfil properly all the essential economic conditions.

It was a masterpiece of understatement to announce the planning of the slowest and smallest ships feasible for the job, and to end up with the two largest vessels in the world. And the eschewing of competition with other companies, as though the Blue Riband had never existed, was also less modest – and less honest – than it sounded. For Cunard knew well that Norddeutscher Lloyd were planning a pair of ships, the *Bremen* and the *Europa* which, before the decade was out, were to sweep the Atlantic speed record effortlessly away from the poor old *Mauretania*. As a successor to the *Île de France*, the Compagnie Générale Transatlantique were planning a liner, the *Normandie*, which *they* intended to be the largest in the world. While the White Star Line, re-purchased from its American owners after the war by the Royal Mail Steam Packet Company, was even more advanced and was about to lay the keel of the *Oceanic*, the very first thousand-footer in history.

So Cunard's inevitable ship – the first of the pair would be launched and tested before the second was embarked upon – came not a moment too soon. By 1931 Cunard's old Big Three were attracting only 47,960 passengers a year

Opposite: from the *Illustrated London News*

THE GIANT LINER'S ANCESTRY: SHIPS OF EVER-INCREASING SIZE.

DRAWN BY OUR SPECIAL ARTIST, G. H. DAVIS, FROM INFORMATION SUPPLIED BY CUNARD WHITE STAR, LTD.

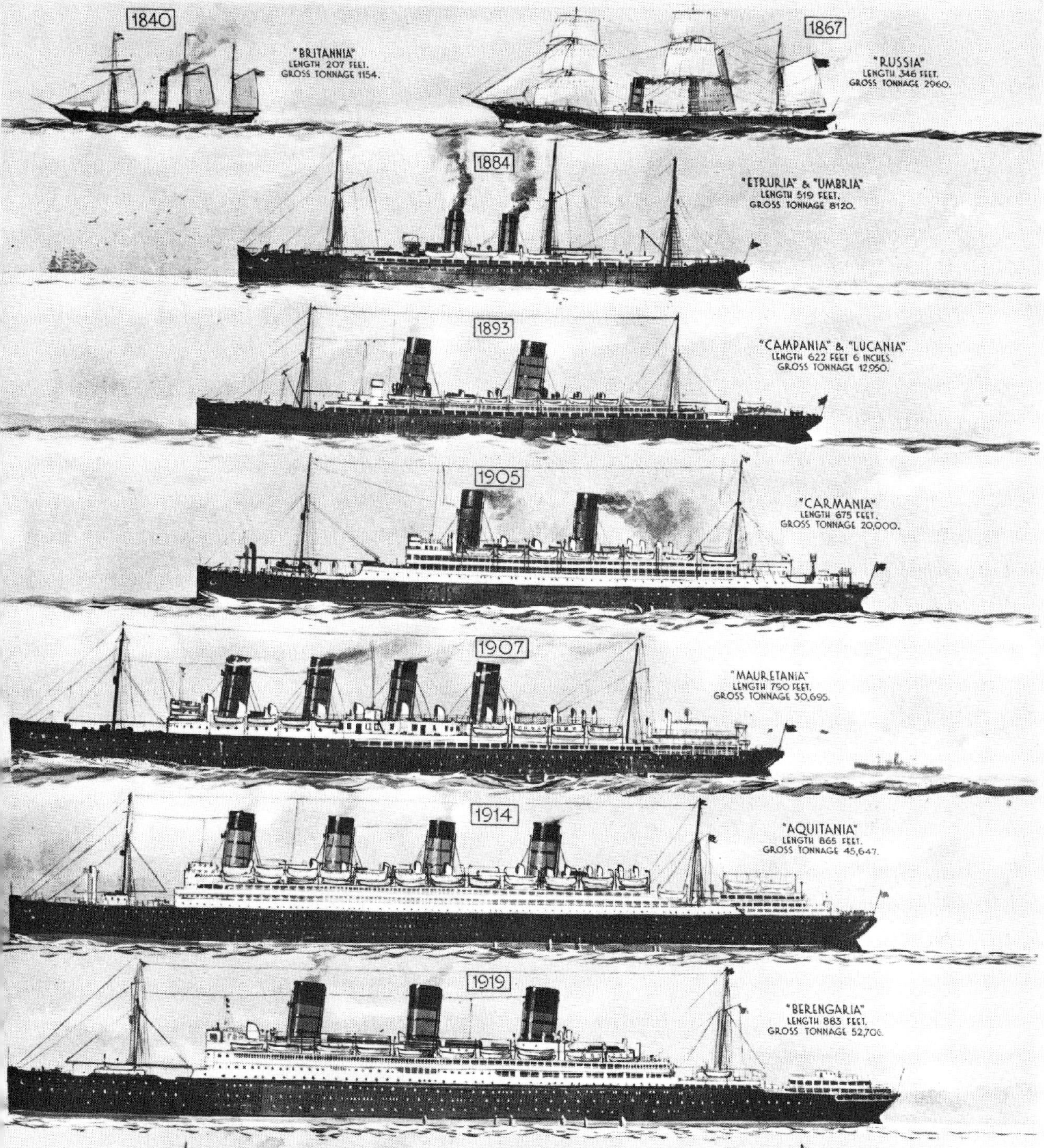

1840

"BRITANNIA"
LENGTH 207 FEET.
GROSS TONNAGE 1154.

1867

"RUSSIA"
LENGTH 346 FEET.
GROSS TONNAGE 2960.

1884

"ETRURIA" & "UMBRIA"
LENGTH 519 FEET.
GROSS TONNAGE 8120.

1893

"CAMPANIA" & "LUCANIA"
LENGTH 622 FEET 6 INCHES.
GROSS TONNAGE 12,950.

1905

"CARMANIA"
LENGTH 675 FEET.
GROSS TONNAGE 20,000.

1907

"MAURETANIA"
LENGTH 790 FEET.
GROSS TONNAGE 30,695.

1914

"AQUITANIA"
LENGTH 865 FEET.
GROSS TONNAGE 45,647.

1919

"BERENGARIA"
LENGTH 883 FEET.
GROSS TONNAGE 52,706.

GREAT NEW CUNARDER

APPROXIMATE LENGTH 1018 FEET.
APPROXIMATE TONNAGE 73,000.

THE CLIMAX OF NEARLY A CENTURY OF SHIPBUILDING PROGRESS: THE HUGE CUNARD WHITE STAR LINER
WITH PREDECESSORS DRAWN TO THE SAME SCALE.

The biggest and the best of everything went into the *Queen Mary* as a matter of principle

compared to 82,017 in 1928 and 87,882 in 1930 – the numbers that the *Bremen* and *Europa* had carried.

And there was another, far more potent threat. On 27 May 1927 Charles A. Lindbergh piloted the single-engined *Spirit of St Louis* from Long Island non-stop to Paris. Lindbergh, in fact, spent a day and a quarter above the Atlantic and he had passed over all the great liners – a forbidding omen, though one which the steamship companies chose to shrug off:

> The simple truth is that aerial transport can never be made to pay. It can only be run on a scale of charges, which, compared with state-room fares, is simply preposterous. There will, probably, always be a very limited number of people prepared to pay these charges, just as there will always be people prepared to face the heavy irreducible risks of flying. The fundamental fact to bear in mind, in regarding the airplane as a commercial proposition, is that four-fifths of her total power must always be expended in keeping her in the air, leaving her only one-fifth to exert on her payable load.

A timetable that the first of the Cunard monsters could adhere to punctually was worked out in the earliest stages of planning:

Westward Passage

Leave	Time	Arrive	Time
Southampton	Wednesday noon		
Cherbourg	Wednesday 6 p.m.	Ambrose Channel	
		Light Vessel	Monday 6 a.m.
		New York	Monday 9 a.m.

Number of hours in New York – 50
Steaming time from Cherbourg to Ambrose – 112 hours

Eastward Passage

Leave	Time	Arrive	Time
New York	Wednesday 11 a.m.		
Ambrose Channel			
Light Vessel	Wednesday 12.30 p.m.		
		Cherbourg	Monday 9.30 a.m.
		Southampton	Monday 3.30 p.m.

Number of hours in Southampton – $44\frac{1}{2}$

Steaming time from Ambrose to Cherbourg – 112 hours

This meant a speed of between 27·61 and 28·94 knots, more than fast enough for the Blue Riband. And the dimensions needed for the 2,000 passengers that would pay for this speed were also record-breaking – 1,018 feet overall length, 118 feet moulded breadth, and a gross tonnage of some 80,000 tons. Cunard directors studied countless plans for housing their passengers, ranging from segregation into four separate classes to the provision of 'hotel liner' facilities in which all public rooms would be shared while passengers would pay according to the location and appointments of their cabin. After studying the market a segregated three class system was decided upon, a First Class, Cabin Class and Tourist, while all would share a single pipe sewage and drainage system – a great saving on weight and expense. Health engineers had previously designed marine plumbing so that sink, bath and basin drainage water was voided into the ocean separately from lavatory waste – the natural anxiety being that the movement of a ship could make for unpalatably mixed back-surges and flows in the event of any blockages. But Cunard engineers, with the help of a scale model sewage system tricked out with pipes filled with appropriately coloured liquids, were able to convince their directors that their one pipe system would be quite safe.

But the main problems that faced the Cunard Steam Ship Company were less the details of the ship itself than the facilities that the vessel could look forward to once it was completed. For Southampton, the intended British terminal, did not possess a dry dock large enough to take her, while the cost of port facilities in New York for a liner of such length was prohibitive. Most awkward of all, no private insurer or group of insurers could be found to cover the several millions of pounds risk that the completed vessel would involve – it was by far the highest risk that Lloyds had ever been asked to insure – so though by the end of May 1930 Cunard felt able to tell John Brown's, the Clydeside ship-builders, that they had been selected to construct the proposed liner – no contract could be signed until the problems of insurance and service facilities had been sorted out.

By now, with the plan for the two great liners public knowledge in Britain, intense interest was centred on the problems that the first of the pair was encountering. Cunard went to the government to ask for help with insuring the vessel, but *The Times*, in a leader dated 22 September 1930, asked:

Is it wise that Parliament should be asked to lend a hand to a project planned on so colossal a scale that private enterprise could not find the means to carry it through? ... The real question is whether so large and so elaborate a masterpiece is really needed to convey passengers across the Atlantic. The possibilities of the vessel's being an economic failure have to be faced ...

It was not the only voice raised in opposition to Cunard's ambitious plans, but it proved, for the moment, ineffective. In December 1930 the Cunard (Insurance) Act was passed, whereby the government assumed the balance of the risk for the

39

liner's value over and above the £2·7 million that the normal insurance market felt able to bear – roughly £1·5 million since the vessel's insurance value during construction was set at over £4 million. But while the government was helpful, private enterprise, in the shape of the Southern Railway Company who owned the docks at Southampton, had proved less tractable. It was essential that there should be accommodation to dry-dock the ship in Southampton for her over-hauls, but the Southern Railway Company was understandably unwilling to commit itself to spending at least a million pounds to provide dry-docking facilities for one vessel that might bring in at the most £5,000 in revenue per year.

It was a difficult situation and Sir Percy Bates responded to it with vigour and cunning. He dropped hints to the Southern Railway about the Gladstone dry dock in Liverpool. *That* could take the new Cunarder, and the railway company there would be most grateful for the revenue the new super liner would bring in. He noisily canvassed the possibility of building an entirely new port on the south coast to teach Southampton a lesson. And, over dinner at the Oriental Club he bluntly told Sir Herbert Walker, the general manager of the Southern Railway Company, 'No dry dock, no ship.' Public – and City – opinion would not respond kindly to this obstruction to plans that involved national prestige and international business confidence, while there was, as a trump card, the Cabinet. Sir Percy instructed his negotiators to make much of Cunard's inability to sign a contract without the assurance of dry dock facilities:

> Use the unsigned contract as a lever with which to move the Government. Nothing must leak out to the Press. We have a difficult game to play with the Government, and publicity of the wrong kind would seriously hamper us in playing it.

The blackmail succeeded. The Government were far from anxious for the great insurance subsidy scheme to be nullified by a single railway company's obstinacy and so Sir Herbert Walker duly bowed to the pressures brought to bear upon him and sanctioned the expenditure of £1·5 million on an immense dry dock 1,200 feet long, 135 feet wide and 48 feet deep. Over in America too, the New York Harbour Authority, faced with the disastrously slumping prices of the depression, felt compelled to come to terms and agreed to construct a special thousand-foot pier which would cost Cunard the comparatively low rent of £48,000 a year. Sir Percy Bates had won through.

Before the end of December 1930 it was possible to drive the first rivet into Hull 534 on Clydeside, and within a month the entire length of the largest keel ever laid in Scotland had been completed. Workmen laboured night and day in three shifts so that the skeleton of the body was towering over the river by spring. And by autumn almost all the plating had been riveted into place, rising high to the decks and flowing all round the vessel's long curved belly. It looked as if a launch before midsummer 1932 and service on the Atlantic by 1934 was possible.

But the Clydesiders toiling over Hull 534 were, in 1931, unusually fortunate beings in a country where fewer and fewer men were taking home pay packets. And the directors of the Cunard Steam Ship Company were, in their boardroom world, even more unusual exceptions to a rule of retrenchment and contraction in the face of economic depression. As 1931 wore on, the question became more urgent and desperate. Could Hull 534 survive the slump?

Opposite: fitted after the *Queen Mary* was launched: the pinion wheels weighing nearly 80 tons

3. HULL 534 ABANDONED

With the 1,000-ft keel laid, Hull 534 takes shape in John Brown's Clydebank yard

Nearly six years after the directors of the Cunard Steam Ship Company had first gathered to plan Hull 534, they met again on Thursday 10 December 1931, and their mood was a less optimistic one. For the first time for years old Sam Cunard's licence to print money on the North Atlantic run had been unable to pay any dividend on its Preference or Ordinary Shares. Hull 534 had already cost £1½ million and Cunard simply did not have the cash for the next million and a half needed to get her launched, let alone the three million pounds she would require to be fitted out ready for service. British earnings from passenger traffic on the North Atlantic had fallen from over £9 million in 1928 to under £4 million in 1931, and given the depressed state of business both in Europe and America the revenues looked like continuing to fall in the foreseeable future.

There was only one possible decision that Cunard could come to, and at seven o'clock next morning, the sad announcement was posted at John Brown's yard. Just a fortnight before Christmas 1931 some 3,500 workers had to go home to their families with the grim news, while the livelihoods of some 10,000 other people were also crippled by the sudden disappearance of the contracts for the steel, electrical equipment, and other machinery that the great liner needed. Hull 534 had for months looked like a skeleton, her bare steel ribcage towering over the grey slate rooftops of Clydeside. Now she was a skeleton in reality, and the families who lived around her became tomb dwellers. Hogmanay was a sad festival in Glasgow in 1931, and life grew sadder through 1932 as Clydebank's M.P., David Kirkwood, described:

> We think of a prison as a place where men are shut in. It is worse than prison for men to be shut out of work. And their wives – those heroic women of the tenement – had seen their men depressed and nervous. They had long ago eaten up their little savings. They had struggled with untold splendour of sacrifice to pay the rent, to keep the husband and children fed and clad; aye, and still more, to keep up the spirit of the men. To them the sight of the closed gate and the horrid framework beyond had been a blight.

By the end of 1932 deputations were petitioning the local Education Committee for extra food for the children of the unemployed.

> It is quite true to say that unemployed people's children go to school with half a slice of bread and margarine and sometimes a drink of tea if there is such a thing in the house. At the dinner hour they come in to a penny bone and a pennyworth of lentils and sometimes a pennyworth of vegetables. At tea time they have bread and margarine once again.

As a result of such a diet – there were no school-meals provided in Scotland in the 1930s – the children were 'so undernourished that they were not even able to pull along the heavy boots which the authority had provided for them with clothing'. Rooks and starlings and a small maintenance staff employed to keep the rust at bay alone gained comfort from the biggest bird's nest in the world.

And in the meantime the Cunard Steam Ship Company was also suffering painfully. While the *Bremen* and *Europa* continued to ply back and forth across the Atlantic earning handsome profits for Norddeutsche Lloyd, the once proud British company ploughed deeply into the red. Hull 534 was not the only sacrifice Cunard had to make. Sir Percy Bates had to announce in 1932, after prolonged negotiations, that every employee of the company, at sea or ashore, had accepted a substantial reduction in salary that would save some £1·78 million a year in operating costs, and that this fierce economy applied 'from the directors down'.

Work begins again: Clydebank workers troop off the ship for their lunch break. Now they could afford to feed their families once more

Weetabix advertisement celebrates the rebirth of the *Queen Mary*. The *Queen Mary* was a symbol of national self-respect – and national virility as well, a source of pride for all and profit for some

4. QUEEN MARY
CHRISTENS HER SHIP

Her identity is a secret no longer. Hull 534
takes to the water as the *Queen Mary*.
But for a misunderstanding on the King's
part she might have been named
Queen Victoria

So it was not only Hull 534 that needed salvation, it was the Cunard Steam Ship Company itself – and the whole British passenger-carrying industry on the North Atlantic, as well. For the White Star Line was also in difficulties and had had to cancel before her hull was started, the great *Oceanic* which had been planned to forestall Hull 534 in the thousand-foot liner stakes. The *Daily Telegraph*, ill-disposed towards government intervention, spoke for Britain as a whole when it argued that so far as Hull 534, Cunard and White Star were concerned, there *was* a case for assistance from public funds. It was a matter of 'national pride' that Britain should be able to hold her head up again on the North Atlantic.

And so in October 1932, nearly a year after John Brown's shipyards had gone dead, Neville Chamberlain, Chancellor of the Exchequer, invited Lord Weir, former Minister of Aircraft Production, to look into the trading and financial health of the British North Atlantic steamer companies – and into the comparative prosperity of their foreign competitors. And Lord Weir's report was completed by the end of the year. Having demonstrated the enormous degree to which foreign governments subsidized the steamship lines that flew their flag, he advised that Cunard should be lent cheap money both for the completion of Hull 534 and for the construction of her sister ship, on the condition that the company should merge with the White Star Line. And this, in fact, corresponded exactly to the plan that Neville Chamberlain had noted in his private diary:

> My own aim has always been to use the 534 as a lever for bringing about a merger between The Cunard and White Star Lines, thus establishing a strong British firm in the North Atlantic trade.

Chamberlain knew that he had on his side what he described as 'that persuasion which naturally arises in those who have the power of the purse'. Neither Cunard nor White Star were disposed to quarrel with an offer of £9½ million at low interest to a new company to be known as Cunard White Star Ltd. Cunard were to own sixty-two per cent of the combine – a fair reflection of the assets they contributed to the merger – and the £9½ million was to be spent in three ways – £3 million to finish 534, £1½ million working capital, and £5 million for a sister ship.

The only problem was Parliament, which had to sanction this huge loan to private enterprise at a time when countless public projects were desperately short of capital. It was not surprising that many Labour members fiercely fighting for government funds for their own constituents should bitterly oppose such a hand-out to a group of capitalists who had got themselves into trouble through their own ambition and greed for profits. But there were also Conservative members who were critical. However, the arguments deployed by David Kirkwood proved, in fact, to be the arguments that saved the day for Hull 534:

> In the deserted hours of the night heavy lorries have been lumbering over distant roads bringing materials from every part of England to Clydebank for the construction of this ship.
>
> Giant castings and forgings have come from English foundries and forges. Seven turbo-generators are being built now in Rugby; they are powerful enough to supply light and public service to a large town. Walsall is sending 400 tons of high-pressure tubes. When the Bill goes through today and the word goes forth to go right ahead with the ship the Potteries will have to make her 200,000 pieces of crockery; Sheffield will have to make her 100,000 pieces of cutlery, having already supplied heavy castings and forges up to a weight of 1,000 tons.
>
> The cases for the rotary turbines, some of the finest casting that has ever been done,

Hull 534 nearly ready for launching. Once afloat she was to be fitted out properly

have come from Sheffield, milled and machined in Clydebank to the limits of 1,000 up and 1,000 down, in which will be placed hundreds and thousands of blades set by hand by Scottish engineers to the thousandth part of an inch. Liverpool has an order for £10,000 worth of glass for myriad windows of the ship. The propellers come from a Millwall foundry in London.

A Darlington forge supplied the stern frame, one of the greatest engineering feats in casting that has been accomplished in the history of the world, a casting weighing 190 tons. When it was leaving Darlington by rail they had to take it on a cylinder and it closed up the whole way. It took six hours to convey it twenty miles to Middlesbrough where it was transhipped. Practically all Darlington turned out to see the wonderful feat of transport of 190 tons along that railway. The casting was then transhipped to the Clyde.

I have seen those pieces in their place. Hundreds of Southampton men have carved out of the earth a dock, the greatest dock in the world, in which the ship may rest, the world's greatest maritime achievement. Among other things that will be required, and these all come from England, are miles of anchor chains, miles of carpets, miles of curtains, and tens of thousands of electric globes and bell pushes. The ship will require equipment for 15,000 meals every day while at sea. From 9,000 to 10,000 men will be employed right away all over the country. Within a week in Clydebank alone anything from 1,000 to 1,500 men will be started.

It was more than a matter of jobs and employment, it was a matter of national pride – as Sir Joseph Nall emphasized in a sad little anecdote:

I well remember, a little over a year ago, coming back from New York in the *Mauretania*. I do not think I have ever felt so depressed at the position which this country seemed to be occupying as, upon a Sunday morning, in a fairly still sea, with a mist,

Queen Mary at launching, watched by her husband King George V, the first time that reigning British royalty had graced the launching of a merchant or passenger ship

Sailing out for trials in the open sea. Britain wanted the Blue Riband snatched at the first opportunity. But Cunard took it cautiously – as ever

the *Mauretania* was running almost parallel with the *Île de France* when away in the mist appeared the *Bremen*, which in an hour had overtaken both ships. The old *Mauretania*, still the fastest of the British ships on the North Atlantic run, was over · twenty-five years old.

The North Atlantic Shipping (Advances) Bill was finally passed on 27 March 1934, and before the week was through letters were going out all over Glasgow.

Dear Sir,

Please report to Messrs. John Brown and Co. Ltd, Clydebank on Tuesday April 3, 1934 at 7.40 a.m. ready to start work. Please hand the enclosed introduction card to employer.

To the skirl of pipers the Clydeside troopers marched back in their thousands to scour off 130 tons of rust and to scare away the colonies of ravens who, for two years and four months, had had the great steel cathedral to themselves. Lloyd's inspectors confirmed that the hull, boilers and machinery were all in excellent order and by the end of that summer Hull 534 was ready for launching.

When, on 26 September 1934, King George V arrived to see her go down the slipway, he made reference to the long slumber from which, Sleeping Beauty-like, she had been awakened by Neville Chamberlain's £9½ million kiss:

Today we come to the happy task of sending on her way the stateliest ship now in being. For three years her unaccomplished hull has lain in silence on the stocks. We know full well what misery a silent dockyard may spread amongst a seaport and with what courage that misery is endured. During those years when work upon her was suspended we grieved for what that suspension meant to thousands of our people.

We rejoice that with the help of my Government it has been possible to lift that cloud and to complete this ship. Now, with the hope of better trade on both sides of the Atlantic, let us look forward to her playing a great part in the revival of international commerce.

It has been the nation's will that she should be completed, and today we can send her forth no longer a number on the books, but a ship with a name in the world, alive with beauty, energy, and strength.

It was the first time that British royalty had deigned to be present at the launching of a merchant ship – and the Poet Laureate duly performed for the occasion. Sir Percy Bates, now the Chairman of Cunard-White Star, had tried to persuade his old friend Rudyard Kipling to roll out one of the patriotic odes at which he was so accomplished, but the great man considered it beneath him to write to order. 'Let Masefield do his own job,' he growled. 'He used to be a sailor.' And so poor Masefield obliged:

. . . a rampart of a ship,
Long as a street and lofty as a tower.
Ready to glide in thunder from the slip
And shear the sea with majesty of power.
I long to see you leaping to the urge
Of the great engines, rolling as you go.
Parting the seas in sunder in a surge

Shredding a trackway like a mile of snow,
With all the wester streaming from your
*   hull,*
And all great twanging shrilly as you race
And effortless above your stern a gull
Leaning upon the blast and keeping place.

This ditty was entitled *Number 534*, because even the Poet Laureate did not know what Cunard's great iron maiden was due to be christened. The newspapers had been full of suggestions – *Clydania, Leonia, Scotia, Britannia, Galicia,* and

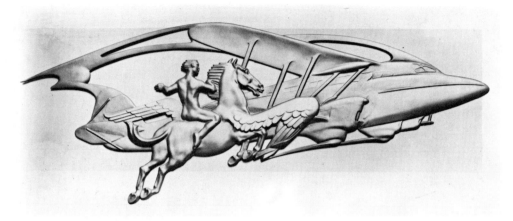

Aluminium motif symbolizing speed. 'The workmanship is magnificent', wrote Cassandra in the *Daily Mirror*, 'the materials used are splendid, and the result is appalling'

Hamptonia – all limping under the weight of the ungainly suffix which Cunard tradition demanded. *Victoria* was the most gracious name that could be contrived within the limits of the '-ia' rule, but this required royal consent, so Lord Roydon, one of the directors of Cunard and a personal friend of George V, undertook to secure His Majesty's permission.

King George had just potted a grouse when his lordship popped the question. Would his Majesty consent to the great liner being named 'after the most illustrious and remarkable woman who has ever been Queen of England,' he asked.

'That is the greatest compliment that has ever been made to me or my wife,' exclaimed the King, lowering his gun. 'I will ask her permission when I get home.'

And so Hull 534 became the *Queen Mary*, and the world heard the name for the first time when Queen Mary herself on 26 September 1934 smashed against the bows of the liner a bottle of Australian wine – champagne would hardly do since it was the recently completed French liner *Normandie* that looked likely to be the *Queen Mary*'s most dangerous rival. Over 200,000 spectators, many of them in specially constructed stands at fifteen shillings a seat, braved relentless, sheeting rain to witness the 100 seconds that the launching lasted:

'There were yards of ermine and gold braid,' said one Scottish observer, 'and a long roster of resounding titles, behind the rain flooded glass of the launching dais. A bottle smashed high upon the precipice that was the port bow of the ship – a curiously feeble sound in the rain-filled space of the yard. Heavy hammers thumped on blocks of wood. Thirty thousand tons of steel, painted white, were moving, nay, plunging toward the water. Chains whipped and lashed like snakes. There was a spurt of flame, dowsed in clouds of oily smoke, over the greased way. She seemed to move at a terrific speed. She was surely rushing to disaster. The army of spectators was silent. Then it liberated itself in a roar. For there was the *Queen Mary*, no longer a number in the books, riding high and light in the narrow river, and the tugs bearing down on her with the purposefulness of terriers after a rat.'

Next day in the fitting-out basin work started on turning the vast empty bath-tub into a ship with engines, fuel tanks, public rooms and accommodation for 2,038 passengers and 1,285 officers and crew. And now began the decor war that was to result in the strange compromise between austerity and vulgarity that was somehow to endear itself – despite their better judgements – to generations of

Altar-piece for chapel, the focus of regular worship. There were facilities for Roman
Catholics – and a synagogue as well

The forward cocktail lounge. The main dining room and foyer had space for the *Britannia*, Cunard's first liner, with Columbus's *Nina*, *Pinta* and *Santa Maria* alongside

State-room corridor, behind whose panelling ran 4,000 miles of cable – enough to reach from New York to San Francisco and 800 miles on out into the Pacific

The Verandah Grill, by day the smartest restaurant, after dark the smartest night club. Passengers paid an additional cover charge for the privilege of eating here

First-class lounge, where you could sit and, according to the experts, be effortlessly propelled across the Atlantic by power equivalent to seven million galley slaves

transatlantic travellers. For though Sir Percy Bates and his directors were determined that their new ship should not be a floating stately home in the tradition of the great pre-war liners, when they saw the results of the modern art that they had commissioned they lost their nerve – with curious results that might have been predicted from the confusions in the original memoranda on the subject:

> When inexpert people like myself express a preference for period architecture, it is, I think, because one is afraid of the bizarre [wrote one director]. If you tell a decorator one would like something modern in a room one feels it is dangerous, because he may feel it incumbent upon him to produce something striking and unrestful.
>
> If, on the other hand, modernism could mean simplification and the replacement of ornate decoration by pleasant and graceful colour schemes with new lighting effects and so forth, then it might prove to be what the travelling public really wants and might, at the same time, save the company a great deal of money.

Samuel Cunard would have applauded that final hope. A 'period ship' would be an expensive ship. A functional, modern ship would be simple and cheap, and this basic economic motive was rationalized into cautious businessman's aesthetics. Cunard's few ventures into serious (and expensive) art justified this caution – to the directors themselves at least. Sir Stanley Spencer turned in a panel depicting a group of riveters straining against a metal plate – not at all the sort of sweaty pastime the Cunard board wished their passengers to be reminded of – while Duncan Grant, commissioned to decorate the lounge, produced paintings which, in the opinion of art critics, represented 'a landmark in the history of decorative art . . . masterpieces,' but which Sir Percy Bates found less historic. When he set eyes on them, he turned his back and walked out of the room.

'You know what you can do with those,' he cried.

'Yes, sir?' said one of his lackeys helpfully.

'Give them to the blind school!' said the Chairman wittily.

In place of the paintings were erected mirrors 'as nice, if not nicer,' said Sir Percy, 'than any pictures.'

'Frankly is it proper and seemly,' enquired Clive Bell in the *Listener*, 'that on a matter of taste some ignorant businessman should be allowed to overrule the best official and unofficial opinion in England?'

But Raymond Mortimer, also in the *Listener*, took a more realistic view.

> For my part I think the mistake was not so much to reject the pictures as ever to commission them.
>
> A super-luxury transatlantic liner depends largely on the patronage of international film stars, financiers and opera singers, and their taste is presumably reflected in the international style of decoration which you find in the palatial hotels all over the world from Palm Beach to the Lido.
>
> I cannot think that such persons would take much notice of Mr Grant's panels, and it would obviously have been unwise not to give them what they prefer.

It was with 'such persons' in mind that Doris Zinkeisen, the toast of the gossip columns and glossy magazines, was commissioned to organize the decor for the Verandah Grill, intended as the meeting point for the élite, 'snob de la snob', of the passenger list 'the centre of sophistication in the ship . . . the rendezvous for the smart set at lunchtime . . . the night club in the evening.' Miss Zinkeisen's reputation rested on the costumes she had designed for such artistic tours de force as Anna Neagle's film *Nell Gwyn*, and her decor lived up to all that was implied by the position she held at one film studio as 'Personality Creator' – responsible for ensuring that starlets appeared in public appropriately clad and made up.

Film-star passengers: Mary Pickford (top), Gracie Fields (left), Marion Davies (right). Their fans waved them farewell – and greeted them in ecstasy on the other side

Hannen Swaffer, one of the more famous journalists to find the *Queen Mary* and her passengers a source of good copy

Pets had their own special quarters – and attendants. There was also accommodation for the serving men and maids brought along by first-class passengers

Boat-drill for the tourist class. Their accommodation was to the rear of the ship over the
propellers. Cabin class were forward; first class in the middle on top

Press conferences for the world-famous: today the photographers haunt the airports.
In the age of the Queens the ocean terminals were their snapping ground

Clive Bell in the *Listener* contrasted the beauty and grace of the ship's marine architecture when seen from the outside with the tawdry mish-mash of styles within, and this was a distinction taken up by *The Architect and Building News*.

There are two architects: the ship architect for the hull and deck and the hotel architect for the inside. The standard of finish and craftsmanship from beginning to end is beyond all criticism. The pictures and sculpture are varied in kind and quality and not all of them fit happily into their setting. The general effect is one of mild but expensive vulgarity.

The lounge, in maple burr and makone, carpeted in green and grey and offset with a great deal of gold is too reminiscent of Oxford Street furniture shops. [This is not surprising, as an Oxford Street firm had done the decoration!]

The dining-room certainly does achieve an atmosphere of richness unequalled by any London hotel.

It is the largest room ever built in a vessel and its architecture would do excellently for an important church.

It was the Winter Gardens effect of the strip-lighting played on so many veneers and plastic laminates which produced the overall impression Clive Bell described as 'teddy-bear' and which others designated as 'Leicester Square'. But Leicester Square was, after all, a resort sought out by millions, revered as a temple of pleasure both by the British native and the transatlantic tourist. And the admiration and enthusiasm with which ordinary passengers, as opposed to art critics, applauded the interior design of the *Queen Mary* in the 1930s must indicate that the directors of Cunard had the appropriate taste for the job. If they knew little about art, they certainly knew what they liked – as Neil Potter and Jack Frost, the great biographers of 'The Mary', testify in their description of the style in which the Trocadero was decked out for five gala dinners to celebrate the birth of the new ship:

The corridor entrance from Shaftesbury Avenue had been pictorially arranged to represent Southampton Docks, and a wall two feet thick had been cut through so that guests could use a regulation gangway to 'go aboard'.

In the restaurant itself there was a captain's bridge and a five-tier deck, built to scale. Searchlights, bells, navigation lights, house flags of the company, and *Queen Mary* lifeboats completed the setting, with the periodic roar of a whistle adding local colour. Guests sat in deck-chairs and were served by waiters dressed as stewards. Sir Edgar Britten, the Cunard Commodore had autographed all the menus. After a cabaret the guests danced in the rays of a searchlight in a salon which took the form of a raft moored to the ship, and the orchestra played from the lifeboats. This was typical of the spirit and age of the *Queen Mary*, for she had so captured the imagination of the nation.

It was only appropriate before the Great Ship sailed that the new King Edward VIII should come for a tour of inspection with the Royal Family, including the two daughters of his brother the Duke of York, the little princesses Elizabeth and Margaret. The King's own comment on the strange mélange of styles that made up the interior of the vessel was a tasteless flannel suit worn with a rakish straw hat. Everyone took this peculiar garb as some sort of compliment to the informality of the liner's modern character.

But old Queen Mary herself saw the point.

'You would not have dared to dress like this, my boy,' she said in a loud voice, 'if your father had been here.'

Opposite: the highest honour from the first voyage to the last: dinner at the Captain's table

5. THE
ULTIMATE SHIP

The launching of the *Queen Elizabeth*, September 1938, by Queen Elizabeth. King George VI could not come – he was awaiting the news from Munich

The *Queen Mary* had the doubtful distinction of being recorded in Lloyd's list of wrecks and casualties on the very first occasion that she sailed. For though the Clyde Navigation Trust had spent eighteen months dredging and widening their river for the moment when the big ship sailed, on the day itself, 24 March 1936, the liner ran aground when a gust of wind caught her stern and scraped her on to the south bank off Dalmuir Light. The Clyde pilot on the bridge said later that his charge had 'skidded' and she was, indeed, stuck for such a short time – just a minute or so – that the thousands of spectators on the banks and eleven circling aeroplanes overhead scarcely realized that anything had gone wrong.

Then, after a pause at the mouth of the Clyde, she was off south for her running trials, which included a record tour of her deck by Lord Burghley, Britain's Olympic sprinter. He covered the 400 yards around the promenade deck in under sixty seconds while wearing evening dress – a feat solemnly recorded by a plaque set up for the admiration, if not the emulation, of First Class strollers.

On 27 May 1936 the *Queen Mary* sailed on her maiden voyage. One artist imagined her travelling up the Thames, somehow escaping the bridges to crash-land in Trafalgar Square:

> her stern has pushed in the walls of the Garrick Theatre in Charing Cross Road; her port side only just fits alongside St Martin's Church and South Africa House; the National Gallery is severely damaged, and her stern has protruded into Whitehall.

Seven million galley slaves all rowing in unison could, it was calculated, barely equal the power of the liner's great turbines. The cables carrying electricity around the ship stretched 4,000 miles – from New York to San Francisco and on 800 miles towards Hawaii. There was room in the main dining room and foyer for old Sam Cunard's *Britannia*, with Christopher Columbus's *Nina*, *Pinta*, and *Santa Maria* alongside for good measure. The tonnage of the ship was over 20,000 tons more than that of the entire Spanish Armada, while the food taken on board for the maiden voyage was enough to feed an army:

Fresh meats	50,000 lb.	Potatoes	50,000 lb.
Poultry	20,000 lb.	Nuts	600 lb.
Fresh Fish	17,000 lb.	Flour	35,000 lb.
Bacon and ham	9,000 lb.	Sugar	20,000 lb.
Sausages	2,000 lb.	Tea and coffee	4,000 lb.
Vegetables	50,000 lb.	Biscuits	1,000 lb.
Fresh fruits	30,000 lb.	Milk	2,000 gallons
Butter and lard	10,000 lb.	Beer	20,000 bottles
Eggs	50,000	Draught beer	6,000 gallons
Ice cream	6,000 quarts	Cigars	5,000
Wines	14,500 bottles	Cigarettes	25,000 packets
General Stores	200,000 lb.		

There were dog kennels on the sports deck – 'All very well,' said Edward VIII, 'but where are the lamp-posts?' – and Mickey Mouse films in the cinema which Princess Elizabeth herself started by pressing the control button. Austin Reed designed a special *Queen Mary* tie complete with a royal purple stripe, price 4s. 6d., available only from their two shops on board. There were Turkish baths

Previous pages: a propeller that was even larger than the *Queen Mary* could boast

to refresh both sexes (separately), and camomile shampoos for lady passengers at 5s. a time (eyebrow arching 2s. 6d., peroxide and olive-oil scalp massage 4s.). In the cargo compartments were 16,000 empty envelopes all stamped 'Per S.S. *Queen Mary*' for the delight and profit of philatelic enthusiasts, and there was also in the hold a Rolls Royce in which Miss Frances Day, the singer hired to croon with Henry Hall's dance band, intended to drive down Broadway. The kitchen department were rather hurt that the much publicized Miss Day chose to bring on board some live hens who were cooped for the voyage alongside the dog kennels. It was most important, explained the lady, that she should have new-laid eggs for breakfast throughout the voyage.

Still, when she sang *Somewhere at Sea*, the signature tune Henry Hall had written specially for the *Queen Mary*, all was forgiven. Poor Henry Hall and his minstrels were kept up to all hours to link up with the exotic broadcasting hours of far-away radio stations. The B.B.C. maintained what was almost a running commentary across the Atlantic from their own studio and the twenty-eight microphone points on board, while over a hundred reporters filed copy back to their newspapers daily. The only problem was that the 1,849 passengers hand-picked for the maiden voyage were so busy themselves using the 700-line internal switchboard and the liner's radio facilities for such purposes as hearing their dog bark back home in Australia that it was almost impossible at times for the media men to get their stories transmitted.

Not that their stories were worth the effort. The Cunard publicity department could not have written less critical puffs or endeavoured so strenuously to avoid the real news – which was that this much vaunted product of Britain's marine engineering rolled like a pig and vibrated at the stern with all the enthusiasm of a pneumatic drill. Within a matter of months the Big Ship was to be withdrawn from service 'for routine overhauls' that involved the total stripping down of the great lounge, smoking room and most luxurious state-rooms while huge steel stanchions, eighteen inches in circumference, were bolted across the top of the liner's wobbly skeleton. Thirty years later Britain was to consider herself mortally disgraced when the turbines of the new *Queen Elizabeth II* were plagued with teething troubles – but those were nothing compared to the comprehensive reconstruction carried out on the *Queen Mary* within a year of her maiden voyage beneath a pall of embarrassed silence.

Right along the entire thousand feet of the liner's hull were fixed twelve- by fourteen-inch channel beams that intermeshed with thick steel cross beams – an incredibly basic, complicated and expensive admission of failure which the press ignored as discreetly as the reason why King Edward VIII did not sail, as had been suggested, on one of the *Queen Mary*'s early voyages. It was not that he disliked the sea. Indeed he spent that very summer cruising in the Mediterranean on Lady Lyle's yacht *Nahlin* with a party of guests that included an American lady, Mrs Wallis Simpson.

Still, in the mid-1930s, newspaper readers had enough to worry about without being burdened with the problems of the ship idolized as a 'symbol of national self-respect', while the silence of passengers who, for example, had had their clothes ruined by smuts and grit blown down on to the deck from the ill-designed smoke stacks, was purchased by Cunard with lavish compensation payments. Smoke-washing filters were installed in the funnels as soon as was practicable.

Thousands of admirers had autographed her great propellors when they had been thrown open for public inspection before being fitted. Now, after only a few voyages, they were sold quietly for scrap while four new screws of entirely different design were installed. It was just as well Percy Bates had got his great dry dock out of the Southern Railway Company for 'routine overhauls'. And even before the *Queen Mary* vanished for her colossal refit, a veritable army of workmen and joiners was ferried to and fro on her across the Atlantic making running repairs, anchoring down furniture that had been running amok on mid-ocean swells, and fixing all along the broad alleyways handrails that made it possible for passengers actually to keep their feet.

Still, the Potteries were happy, for the *Queen Mary* smashed so many sets of her own special china service that extra shifts had to work to keep pace with her demand for replacements. As quickly as new crocks arrived, so they were broken.

Not that she – or her engineers – were entirely to blame. For much of the superficial damage to her fine veneers and mirrors on her early voyages was caused by souvenir hunters. When she docked in New York at the end of her maiden voyage enterprising Americans were on hand to sell specially manufactured mementoes – medallions, pen-and-pencil sets, and so on. But passengers and visitors to the shop were too busy helping themselves to the real thing – ashtrays, tea services, knives, forks, spoons, brass notices and nameplates, pepper-pots and salt cellars, even potted plants and paintings. The welcome that New York gave the *Queen Mary* was extravagant – a fleet of escorting aeroplanes and small ships, water spouts and ticker tape, letters and telegrams by the thousand – but by the time the last visitor had left, the liner looked as though she had been struck by a plague of locusts.

There was a certain disappointment when she got back to Britain that she had not, in Teutonic fashion, seized the Blue Riband on her maiden voyage. But that was remedied by the end of August 1936 when she made the very first Atlantic crossing in under four days – 3 days, 23 hours and 57 minutes from Ambrose Light to Bishop Rock. Almost apologetically Sir Percy Bates explained:

> While we have let out the *Queen Mary* during this voyage we had an object in what we were doing. We are at the moment engaged in consideration of the details of the *Queen Mary*'s sister ship. To help us to a proper consideration of the details of the machinery and the propellers the round voyage such as the *Queen Mary* has run this last fortnight was of the greatest assistance.
>
> Accordingly, before the ship started on the last voyage I took counsel with the builders and our own technical experts, and the figures which we have obtained as a result of this voyage will be of the greatest assistance in considering No. 552 in the next few weeks.

No. 552 was the *Queen Elizabeth*, still just a drawing board design with two funnels, but already taking bookings for her maiden voyage. With £5 million of government money guaranteed, her construction was not a matter of if, but of when and how. And the very major faults that had marred the initial sailings of the *Queen Mary* for her owners and passengers, if not for the media and the public at large, meant that there would be significant improvements and refinements upon her sister ship – in deck allocation, for a start. There had been criticism of the fact that tourist class passengers on the *Queen Mary* could, from their deck space just behind the bridge, look down on first class passengers taking their ease on the boat deck. Vice versa might have been tolerable, but to have the hoi-polloi gawping down on the devotees of the Verandah Grill was a social impropriety of major proportions. Having two funnels rather than three gave the designers deck space with which to avoid this gaffe in the future.

For the energetic the gym complete with mechanical horse which, in 1953, 'threw' Archbishop Fisher of Canterbury

For the contemplative: the library. But most of the books stayed locked up – the library never had the pulling power of shuffleboard

The first-class lounge of the *Queen Elizabeth* duplicated the most successful characteristics of her sister ship – notably the Verandah Grill

The first complete cinema on board a Cunarder. The *Queen Mary*'s passengers had had to make do with drawn curtains in the lounge, home-movie style

Then there was the problem of the *Normandie*. It appeared when the tape measures were got out that the French ship was actually a few inches – or centimetres – *longer* than the *Queen Mary*. So some twelve feet – four metres – were added to the *Queen Elizabeth* to make sure she was quite definitely the largest liner in the world – 1,031 feet overall. And a Cunard engineer was sent to travel on the *Normandie* as a spy, his interminable questions to the crew about shaft horsepower, reduction geared turbines, and boiler pressures somewhat undermining the credibility of his claims to be a grocer. In 1937, in fact, the *Normandie* won back the Blue Riband, getting her crossing time down to 3 days, 22 hours, and 7 minutes – a speed of over 31 knots, so until the *Queen Mary* struck back in August 1938, with 3 days, 20 hours, and 40 minutes (31·69 knots) the mechanical power of the *Queen Elizabeth* was a crucial matter.

On 6 December 1938 keel 552 was laid in John Brown's Clydeside yard, and by the end of the following January the hull was starting to rise. Her bow raked more sharply than that of the *Queen Mary*, and she had just one single flush main deck instead of the little well deck which her sister, and most other contemporary ships, had jutting up at the front. Aesthetically this made for cleaner, faster-looking lines, and though in point of fact the *Queen Mary* was always the faster of the pair, the accent of the *Queen Elizabeth*'s design and decor was throughout on somewhat more grace and light than characterized the parlour heaviness of her sister. The captain's cabin, for example, was veneered a delicate shade of grey with rare wood whose origins were explained by a special plaque:

> The timber used for the lining of this cabin, though botanically known as *Ulmus Americanus*, or Rock elm, has the popular designation of Waterloo elm. It was obtained from the piles driven in 1911 under the original Waterloo Bridge over the river Thames. The change to grey was caused by the bleaching action of tidal waters and discovered when the piles were withdrawn in 1936 to prepare for the new bridge.

The veneer in the main lounge was Canadian maple-burr which made for a beige-pink effect that was set off by panels of light grey, pale blue and beige leather, while the Art Deco motifs presiding over the staircases and artificial fireplaces were made of materials actually employed in the construction of the ship – steel, copper, bronze, aluminium, lead, white metal, glass, and rubber.

Queen Elizabeth, when she came in September 1938, like her mother-in-law four years before her, to launch her ship, was proud to call her 'the noblest vessel ever built in Britain'. And the title Cunard gave their new liner – 'the ultimate ship' – remains valid to this day. For though modern ship-builders could obviously improve on the *Queen Elizabeth*, they will never be given a chance. She was the last of the thousand-foot passenger carriers built before the Second World War, and by the time that war was over the world – and the North Atlantic in particular – was a very different place.

She was launched, indeed, as Neville Chamberlain was flying to Munich to see Hitler, and, in those dark hours of crisis, the King – George to his subjects, Bertie to his family and friends – felt he should stay in London and hand over the speech he had prepared to his wife to deliver. So Queen Elizabeth spoke to the small crowd gathered for the launching (John Brown's were by then working on top-security defence contracts which restricted access) of 'Divine Providence' which, she hoped, 'would bring order out of confusion and peace out of turmoil'.

They were stirring sentiments, stirringly expressed. But, not for the first time, old Queen Mary had the last word. 'She made her speech admirably,' she noted of her daughter-in-law's performance. 'Bertie's really . . .'

6. WAR COMES TO THE NORTH ATLANTIC

The *Queen Elizabeth* in camouflage paint secretly leaves the Clyde on her dramatic maiden voyage with a skeleton crew

War found one Queen an unfinished shell anchored in the River Clyde, and the other steaming in the North Atlantic. The *Queen Elizabeth* was still in her fitting-out basin, a sitting target for any German bomber that could reach the west coast of Scotland, and, more seriously, taking up valuable dock space that was urgently needed for fitting out the battleships of the Royal Navy. The *Queen Mary* was full as never before, bearing a record load – 2,332 passengers, most of them Americans, returning rapidly from the horrors about to strike Europe. When Neville Chamberlain broadcast on the morning of 3 September 1939 the sad news that Britain was at war, the *Queen Mary* was but a few hours out of New York.

And once safely inside the Hudson River the *Queen Mary* stayed there. She disembarked her passengers, most of her crew were sent home in planes or other ships, and all reservations for the return passage or any more sailings were cancelled. She spent the autumn and winter of the 'Phoney War' tied up to Cunard Pier 90 with search-lights playing on her – for though the U-boats of the Atlantic run could not threaten her, Nazi saboteurs could. In the autumn of 1939 New York was not the safest of havens for one of the most prestigious targets Hitler could aim at, and U.S. Intelligence warned Cunard that German agents taking advantage of America's neutral status might attempt to plant bombs on the *Queen Mary*.

But the real problem was less the *Queen Mary* moored in the Hudson River, than the *Queen Elizabeth*, an embarrassingly uncompleted hulk in the Clyde. There was an urgent need to re-equip the battleship *Duke of York* in John Brown's yard, but the *Elizabeth* occupied the fitting-out basin and, in her present state, was scarcely fit to be moved. Unless building were taken a stage further on her she would be no more use than so much scrap. And so, on 2 November 1939, the Ministry of Shipping granted a special licence to allow precious war materials and labour to be devoted to a vessel that was essentially a peace-time pleasure craft. There was no question of decking out the *Queen* with all the luxury planned for her, but to get the bare essentials of electrical and joinery work completed. On 6 February 1940 Cunard were told that the First Lord of the Admiralty, Mr Winston Churchill, had decided that their flagship 'should keep away from the British Isles so long as this order is in force', while from Scotland the tide-tables dictated the precise moment at which the *Queen Elizabeth*'s exile should begin. For there were in 1940 but two occasions when the tides on the Clyde would be high enough for a vessel of the *Queen Elizabeth*'s bulk to be navigated safely down the river to the open sea. One would be on 26 February, the other six months later.

In February 1940 no one could foresee to quite what a pass Britain would be reduced in those next momentous six months. But it was obvious that the situation was critical at that very moment, and that the *Duke of York* could not wait six months for her refit to begin. Since the *Duke of York* was a large ship as well, the *Queen Elizabeth*'s timetable would have to be even more precise. For on 26 February 1940 there would be just two tides high enough to float both vessels. The *Queen Elizabeth* would have to sail out of the fitting basin on the first tide, and the *Duke of York* come in on the second. There was no room for error.

The ultimate destination of the *Elizabeth* once she left the Clyde was also determined by events. There was, obviously, not a single port in Europe to which she could sail, and she had been designed for just one harbour on the other side of the Atlantic. She was not built for runs to Capetown, let alone Singapore or Sydney, safe outposts of the British Empire in these years before Japan entered the war. And she had, besides, never crossed an ocean in her life. Once she had passed beyond the submarine nets at the mouth of the Clyde she would have to make a lightning dash across the Atlantic, her speed tests and navigation tests all part of one deadly serious practical mission. The safest course to follow was the one she was designed for, the ocean passage to New York.

Yet though New York was, of course, an obvious refuge, U-boats were already taking a heavy toll of merchant ships on the Atlantic run. A good cover story would be needed to camouflage the *Queen Elizabeth*'s destination, for there would be no way of hiding her once she started moving down the Clyde. Admiral Doenitz's wolf packs would have to be persuaded to lie in ambush in the wrong place.

So in the early months of 1940 great packing cases containing the *Queen Elizabeth*'s supplies and finishing fittings arrived in Southampton. The King George V dry dock there was reserved for checks on her rudder and propellers. Southampton hotel rooms were reserved for the technicians who would be monitoring her proving trials. And Captain Jack Townley with a crew of 400, most of them from the *Aquitania*, was signed on to take the liner down around the coast to the southern port.

The harbour officials at Southampton were certainly taken in completely, for they wrote to Cunard to ask for a docking plan that Mr McEwan, the Assistant Naval Architect, had hurriedly to concoct. And though Britain was as unlikely to float the world's largest torpedo target up and down the English Channel while one side was in enemy hands as she was to fly hot air balloons to Berlin, on the day that the *Queen Elizabeth* was expected in the Solent the skies were duly filled with Goering's bombers. The decoy had succeeded.

Not that the brief February hours of daylight up on the Clyde passed without anxiety. To make her less visible from the air, the world's most glamorous liner was painted a dull battleship grey. Her forward funnel, which had been already decked out in Cunard's black and red bands, had been repainted, as had her shining white superstructure, while the flanks of the ship were cluttered with over five miles of cable wound round and round as a 'de-gaussing' or anti-mine device. It was a drab sequel to the champagne and ceremony of her launching, but the sight of the sober-sided monster drifting silently out of her fitting basin was a moving and exciting one. To lighten her as much as possible all her lifeboats had been lowered into the water and sailed down the river to wait at the Tail of the Bank. But this same precaution had not prevented the *Queen Mary* from running aground on her maiden voyage, and now the *Queen Elizabeth* had a couple more inches draught and over 2,000 extra tons to negotiate along the same tricky fifteen miles. Getting her vast bulk out cleanly in time for the *Duke of York* to sail safely back up the river would call for both excellent seamanship and good luck.

At lunchtime on 26 February 1940, four hours before high water, the tugs began nudging the 340 yards of ship out into midstream. Over a million spectators had watched the *Queen Mary* make this same brief but demanding trip. Now there were only a few hundred ship-builders and fitters to witness the start of a journey that was to prove even more momentous and tense. For just off the Rashilee Light, at almost the same spot that the *Queen Mary* had gone aground, the incoming tide caught the bows of the *Queen Elizabeth*. For nearly an hour she stood still as the tugs fought to regain control over her, and, as they struggled, the crowds standing on the banks grew, for the word had run through the yards that the pride of the Clyde was on the move. As the tugs pushed and pulled, men all along the river laid down their tools to watch the great grey ship, and the little craft tied by strings to her, battle with the cold waters flowing in from the sea.

And it took fifty minutes of furious manoeuvring by the tug captains all around the stern of the liner to get the big boat's bows biting back into the tide again. As darkness fell at a quarter past five that evening, the *Queen Elizabeth* was finally anchored safely off the Tail of the Bank, having started her maiden voyage with a speed of less than three miles an hour over the first fifteen miles. She would have to travel at more than ten times that speed to survive the next three thousand.

But Captain Jack Townley still had not been told officially what his destination was. A King's Messenger, he was informed, would deliver his orders before the time set for sailing. The crew were told the news that the liner was not in fact sailing to Southampton and that their articles of voyage would have to be changed from coastal to oceanic regulations – but the identity of the port they were heading for remained a mystery. And when a few of the sailors pointed out – reasonably – that they had not signed up for a transoceanic trip they were put on a tender and sailed up into the middle of Gareloch to wait in isolation there until the liner was safely away out in the Atlantic. Those who stayed on board got £30 on top of their wages as 'inconvenience money'.

At seven o'clock in the morning of 2 March 1940, only one hour before the *Queen Elizabeth* was due to sail out through the anti-submarine boom, the long awaited King's Messenger finally arrived with the sealed orders that were not to be opened until the liner was at sea. Four destroyers and an escort of seaplanes and aircraft watched over her zig-zag course until she was 200 miles west of Rathlin Island, and then she was all on her own, steaming for dear life the course to New York that her sealed orders had set for her.

Speed and secrecy were the *Queen Elizabeth*'s only defence. There were some sandbags and a couple of pill boxes on her bridge, but that was all. The Royal Navy would broadcast to Captain Townley news of any German surface or submarine vessels, but his firmer hope of safety lay in the total wireless silence he was under strict orders to maintain. If he was spotted by any enemy U-boats or battleships – the *Deutschland* was thought to be somewhere north west of Ireland – he would just have to dodge their torpedoes and shells with his superior speed and manoeuvrability – the very qualities of his ship that had never been tested at sea and of which he knew nothing. He was a greyhound dashing through a pack of wolves – far speedier and sprier, but a greyhound who had never trained or exercised for the course.

Capable of over thirty knots, either Queen could run rings round any ship that the Germans might have lying in wait. Ten knots was the most that U-boats could manage under water, and they could only attack in calm weather. But the *Queen Elizabeth* would have to try to maintain her top speed without pause.

On board, patrolling in twos and threes the open avenues of the promenade deck, the crew had the impression of being on a *Marie Celeste* – 'a phantom ship steered by phantom hands'. Instead of the full complement of 1,296 crew there were just 398 men aboard – with the facilities for 2,260 passengers to themselves. There was not a company director or millionaire voyager in sight. The crew had a menu printed every day on the ship's presses and had a state-room each in which to sleep in luxurious seclusion. Good fun, like playing hide-and-seek in school when everyone else has gone home, but 'an eerie experience', according to Robert Stein, one of the Glasgow engineers brought along to check the equipment.

On the morning of 7 March 1940 a T.W.A. airliner flying some forty miles east of Fir Island in New York Bay saw a giant ship below her, zig-zagging furiously although she was safely in American waters. The vast decks were empty save for two men at the stern, many of her stairways were unpainted, there were great patches of rust where her hastily applied grey blanket had peeled and the sixty-eight-foot long name letters on her bow had been painted over. But there was no doubt who she was. New York journalists had anticipated the arrival of the *Queen Elizabeth* from the preparations on Cunard Pier 90 the previous day, and on the morning of 7 March there were ten thousand people waiting at the docks – with 100 New York City detectives among them. The first ship to greet the 'Empress Incognito', as the *New York Post* described her, was the sludge dredger *Coney Island*, and she gave the signal for a great chorus of whistles.

> As she slowly made her way up river, she was accorded the tumultuous welcome befitting the most distinguished representative of maritime royalty ever to reach America's shores. Thousands of spectators thronged the windows and tops of West Side buildings. More than a dozen planes circled overhead and dipped time and time again in salute, while scores of tugboats churned the water on all sides of the great grey Majesty with whistles and sirens wide open. The waterfront personnel took to the piers en masse to watch her pass.
>
> *– New York Post*

At a quarter to five in the evening, the big ship finally eased into her berth, her 'new epic of sea adventure' completed. 'Many sagas of the sea have begun and ended in our harbour,' wrote the *New York Times*, 'but can the old-timers remember anything to compare with the unheralded arrival of the biggest and fastest liner in the world, after the most daring of all maiden crossings?'

Could they remember either when two such enormous sister ships had lain alongside each other at one time on the Hudson River? For the *Queen Elizabeth* was tied up right beside the *Queen Mary* at Pier 90. The Queens of the North Atlantic were together at last – and for the very first time.

Together for the first time – the two Queens (the *Elizabeth* in the foreground) berthed alongside the Cunard Company Pier in New York. Beside the *Mary* is the *Normandie*

7. THE QUEENS OF THE SOUTH PACIFIC

The first meeting at sea
– the Queens off Sydney Head, Australia. Both
were operating as troop carriers

For a fortnight the sisters bobbed side by side in the shadow of Manhattan, two vast and echoing arks emptied of the human cargo that gave them weight and life and purpose, the *Queen Elizabeth* in her grey distemper, the *Queen Mary* still sporting her red and black livery with a pride that, in the spring of 1940, was poignant. For U-boats had displaced the Queens as rulers of the North Atlantic and so beside the Queens, rising and falling emptily with them on the spring tides of the Hudson, lay the other great intercontinental ferries, the *Île de France*, *Normandie*, *Aquitania* and *Rex*, redundant until some wartime function could be found.

It was the *Queen Mary* who was the first of the liners to start a new life. The painters arrived in March 1940 to envelop her in the same monotone as her sister, removal men whisked her more portable furnishings into Cunard depositories, the sand suckers cleared the silt of half a year's idleness from beneath her keel, and on 21 March she disappeared from the Hudson River with as much discretion as a thousand-foot-long lady can muster. She had been called up for the service of His Majesty's Government and her destination and course were secret.

Early in April 1940, as she steamed into Table Bay with an escort of bombers, the inhabitants of Cape Town found out where she had been for the previous five weeks – crossing the South Atlantic that she had never sailed before. And South Africans could make an educated guess as to the port that must be her ultimate objective. For south of the Equator only Sydney and Singapore had the harbour facilities properly to look after a vessel of the *Queen Mary*'s size, and in Australia there was a very good reason for re-equipping her – the thousands of men there ready to fight on behalf of that continent's mother country. Built as a bridge between the two oldest components of the English speaking world, the *Queen Mary* was now to unite and strengthen it even further by acting as a troop-ship to bear the fighting men of the Empire to the European theatre of war.

The Cockatoo Docks and Engineering Company were waiting for her when she reached Sydney on 17 April 1940, and in less than two weeks almost trebled her passenger carrying capacity. Into the *Queen Mary* went berths for 5,500 soldiers: wooden bunks in the state-rooms and cabins, hammocks in the public rooms, and those serried ranks of W.C.s without which no barracks, even a floating one, can feel complete.

On 5 May 1940 the converted liner took on board the first 5,000 of the million and a half soldiers who were in the next five years to enjoy the experience of crossing an ocean in a Queen free of charge. In fact, the total number of fare-paying passengers that the two Queens carried barely touched a million each, so it is, perhaps, pre-eminently as troop-ships that we should remember them.

But in May 1940 victory was still very far away. After Dunkirk, Britain had become an island fortress, desperately in need of all the reinforcements that the great steel whales of the liner routes could carry to her in their bellies. And so, sailing across the Indian Ocean with the *Queen Mary* in May 1940, were the *Aquitania*, *Mauretania*, *Empress of Japan*, *Empress of Canada*, and *Andes*, competing palaces of pleasure converted by the direness of the emergency and the shipfitter's grey paint brush from being rivals into an earnest and elephantine convoy of friends.

The *Queen Elizabeth* arrived in Sydney in February 1941 to be refitted. This Pacific reunion of the North Atlantic Queens was an historic one, for on 9 April 1941 the two ships took to the open sea together for the very first time. But the joint service that they started operating in this southern autumn and northern spring was hardly what the Cunard planners had envisaged some fifteen years earlier. For Sydney and Suez were the end points of the service the sisters now operated, taking Australian reinforcements across the Pacific and Indian Oceans to the Desert War. And every trip they made traversed the Equator. So all the trouble that the *Queen Mary* had experienced on her first Australian-bearing voyage was now repeated and intensified as the ships crossed the Arabian Sea and went up the Red Sea without the air conditioning needed to cope with trips in the tropics. They were built to keep passengers snug and warm against North Atlantic gales, and the torrid heat of the Middle East defeated their ventilation systems entirely, turning them into great cauldrons in which their overcrowded passengers boiled. As anxious men neared the battle front, after weeks confined closely together with the sun blazing down remorselessly, tempers frayed – and the liners' crews became fractious too. It was over a year since most of them had been home, and after months of unknown harbours and routes that had turned their fetid quarters in the bowels of the ship into torture chambers, they erupted into the nearest the Queens ever came to mutiny. Having worked out their frustrations on each other with battles that involved saucepans of boiling water, the crew of the *Queen Elizabeth* then revolted against the wartime menus that they were offered by bundling a defenceless cook into his own – heated – oven. The poor man survived, but his attackers were rounded up in the lounge which, in the absence of a roundhouse, served as a prison, and a squad of Royal Marines with bayonets fixed came on board from the escorting cruiser *Cornwall*. The mutineers were taken back to the *Cornwall*, locked up and put ashore at Cape Town whence they were shipped back to disciplinary action in England.

All through 1941 the Queens plied the Sydney to Suez shuttle, virtually unprotected, and then on 7 December 1941 the bombers of Nippon darkened the skies over Pearl Harbour and the entire complexion of the war was transformed. For with the entry of Japan into the conflict the Pacific could no longer be treated as a British lake, and with the entry of America, there was created a vast new clientèle for the Queens to transport. By New Year's Day 1942 new American jobs had been arranged for the sisters, the *Queen Mary* intended for New York and the *Queen Elizabeth* for San Francisco – though for their initial voyages their destinations were the same, Australia again.

Now in 1942, however, their mission was to bear reinforcing troops *to* that island and not away from it. For the Japanese were advancing down the Malay Peninsula like a jungle fire that sprang from Singapore across the Malacca Straits and through the islands of Indonesia. Having weakened herself voluntarily by giving so generously to Britain of her fighting men, Australia was now seriously threatened, and to her in the early months of 1942 the Queens rushed some 20,000 U.S. troops.

The giantesses' changing destinations marked the flow of the world-wide battle – and altered its course as well. With Australia securely defended they could return to New York and begin the transatlantic ferrying which was their métier, and which was to occupy them for the rest of the war. For the next three years, with their identities smothered by grey paint, military discipline and code numbers instead of names, they were to become not so much the Queens of the North Atlantic as the G.I. ferries.

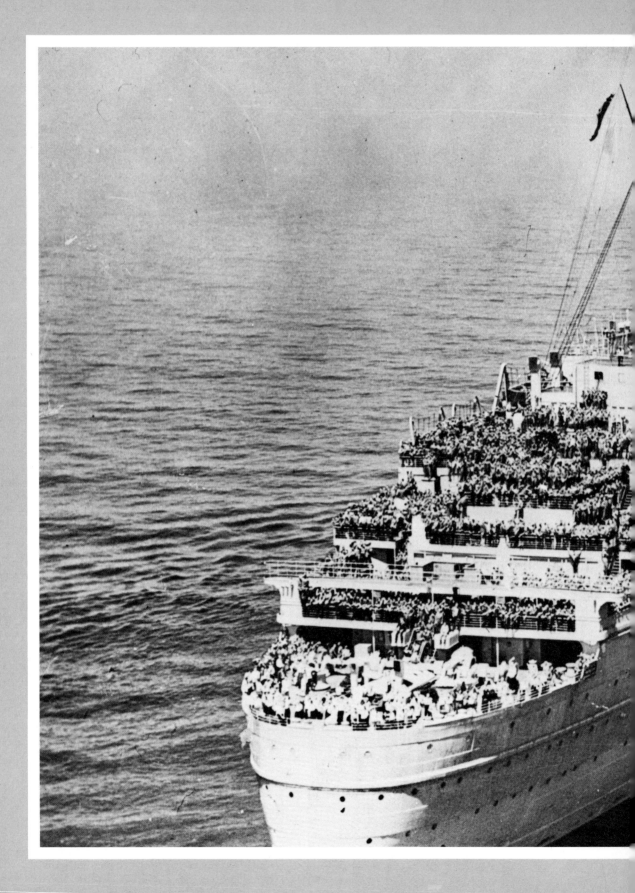

8. THE G.I. FERRIES

Packed to more than capacity with
15,000 troops, the *Queen Mary*
carries G.I.s to Europe

It was impossible, of course, ever totally to camouflage the Queens' identities. They were the largest liners in the world – and the American army reacted to their size in characteristic style. For the two ships, instead of now carrying just the 2,000 or so passengers for which they were intended, or even the 5,000 or so souls that the Australians had managed to cram into each ship, started in the summer of 1942 to bear over 15,000 G.I.s on each voyage that they undertook from New York eastwards. The capacity of the American military authorities to think big amazed even Winston Churchill who, at the beginning of 1942, was in Washington arranging with President Roosevelt such details of the Anglo-American alliance as the use to which the great liners should be put.

> One evening General Marshall came to see me and put a hard question. He had agreed to send nearly 30,000 American soldiers to Northern Ireland. We had, of course, placed the two Queens, the only two 80,000-ton ships in the world, at his disposal for this purpose.
> General Marshall asked me how many men we ought to put on board, observing that boats, rafts and other means of flotation could only be provided for about 8,000. If this were disregarded they could carry about 16,000.
> I gave the following answer. 'I can only tell you what WE should do. You must judge for yourselves the risks you will run. If it were a direct part of an actual operation we should put all on board they could carry. If it were only a question of moving troops in a reasonable time we should not go beyond the limits of the lifeboats, rafts etc. It is for you to decide.'

George Marshall, true to the traditions of America's armed forces, opted for an operation on the most massive scale possible. In May 1942 the *Queen Mary* steamed out of New York heading eastwards, and in August the *Queen Elizabeth* set off on the same course, both liners taking their maximum capacity cargoes to the Clyde which was, for the next three years, to be their eastern terminus.

In war some things at least become simpler, for in this crucial year of 1942 the British government just handed over the two Queens to America without payment of any sort, leaving it to Washington to use and organize the liners as best suited U.S. interests – with the British government meeting all the costs of operating the liners. Cunard were asked to provide crews and to pay them their normal salaries and wages, which the British Government then reimbursed in full along with all fuel, pilotage and docking expenses incurred. America had only to provide the soldiers who sailed on the ships with food and bedding.

It was some compensation for the generosity of Lend-Lease, and the essence of the agreement between the two nations in respect of their resources in general was that either of them could take from the other to help the common cause. By giving away the great liners as G.I. ferries Britain lost valuable troop-carrying capacity, but gained enormously in other ways, for the four American divisions that the *Queen Mary* and *Queen Elizabeth* transported to Northern Ireland in the summer of 1942 enabled trained soldiers to leave the British Isles for the Middle East and to make a decisive contribution to the victory of El Alamein.

The Queens' new masters were both ambitious and ingenious, the device by which they managed to convert the two liners into rabbit warrens being a particular gem of American technology – the standee bunk. This was a one-sided christmas tree of light tubular metal, from whose main supports twelve chains suspended six thin shelves one above the other. The shelves could, when necessary, be flapped up out of the way or, when let down, stack six recumbent G.I.s

Boat drill on the foredeck of the *Queen Mary* – there were life boats for less than half the 15,000 troops the liners carried in summer

G.I. passenger: Colonel James Stewart on the *Queen Elizabeth* which, on one westbound voyage, carried 4,000 wounded G.I.s home in cots or on crutches

one above the other. The Australians had filled the liners with hammocks and wooden bunks, but the Americans worked out that many more men could be crammed into the same space by stacking the standee metal berths tightly on top of each other. And so in the cocktail bar, in the drained swimming pool, in all the cabins, and in every spare nook and cranny of each Queen a metallic forest of struts and chains carried the racks into which G.I.s squeezed twice every twenty-four hours – for sleeping, like eating, was done in shifts. Every standee had assigned to it each day two soldiers who took it in turns to sleep, and when the Queens were especially crowded three men were rotated at the rate of one every eight hours.

G.I.s were also shifted according to the location of their beds within the ship, for in the summer thousands of hammocks were slung up outside on the decks. And so, on every summer voyage, each passenger tasted the pleasures of sleeping *al fresco* at least once – an experience denied to travellers in the winter months when the promenade deck could be chilly to a degree an Eskimo would not relish.

So 15,000 in summer and 10,000 in winter were set as the liners' maximum carrying capacities, and on the summer voyages G.I.s really had to bolt their food. Six thirty in the morning was when the first sitting for the first main meal began, and six, seven or even eight other shifts then followed on at the rate of one every forty-five minutes. As they left the dining room soldiers took sandwiches to last them through the day, for their next meal would not be for another twelve hours when, around tea-time, the shifts began again. Up in the Cabin Class dining room several hundred officers sat at the Cunard captain's tables and enjoyed waiter service and four course meals but down in the galleys the cooks coped with even vaster mountains of food than they had learnt to tackle in peacetime – 30,000 eggs to boil every breakfast with ham machines slicing twenty-four hours a day.

There was a one-way-traffic system devised to keep up to 15,000 men moving efficiently: to move forward, G.I.s took the starboard passageways, and coming back the port side, military policemen supervising the entire system rigidly. On the *Queen Mary* police headquarters were in the Austin Reed shop.

The long twelve hours between main meals could weigh heavy on soldiers confined in the mazes of standee racks, and so concerts and film shows were held every day. All the regiments had their bands and barrack room comedians who could string together concert parties, but the films screened every voyage came out of a small and unchanging stock – which did not matter to the ever changing military passengers, but which meant that at least one Cunard staff member saw *Pride and Prejudice* 120 times.

Soldiers were also given during the day lectures on the British way of life and a list of some important 'Do's and Don'ts' about the correct way to fraternize with the ordinary people of Britain:

> You are higher paid than the British 'Tommy'. Don't rub it in. Play fair with him. He can be a pal in need. It isn't a good idea to say 'bloody' in mixed company in Britain – it is one of their worst swear words. To say 'I look like a bum' is offensive to their ears, for to the British this means that you look like your own backside. The British are beer-drinkers – and they can hold it.

> – *Short Guide to Britain, Special Service Division, U.S. Army.*

Officers, who enjoyed in their own areas of the ships a degree of service from the Cunard stewards, were given further advice on how much to tip at the end of the voyage. Bedroom and table stewards should get one dollar from single officers and 1·50 dollars from officers who had brought their wives or families with them.

British officers who might happen to be travelling on the liners had to pay their cabin steward five shillings if they held the rank of major or above – but captains and lesser fry were let off with four shillings and sixpence.

For six days America's fighting men queued for their meals and beds, listened to their orientation lectures and watched *Pride and Prejudice*, while up on the bridge the Cunard captain kept his craft zig-zagging without even once, in three years' ferrying by both Queens, spotting an enemy warship, plane, U-boat or torpedo. Then a hundred miles or so off the coast of Ireland British cruisers or destroyers would appear and escort the liner for her last few hours of zig-zagging past the Giant's Causeway, round Rathlin Island and down the North Channel to the Firth of Clyde, where, once inside the submarine nets, she was safe. Waiting at the Tail of the Bank would be a flotilla of little pleasure craft and these would swarm out to nestle up to the ship like piglets round a sow while for thirty-six hours ten, twelve, or fifteen thousand G.I.s disembarked, surrendering their great liner to another army – a fierce regiment of cleaning ladies ferried out on a tender with their buckets and mops at the ready.

In a few hours the ship would be cleaned – most stores for the round voyage had been taken on board in New York to avoid Britain's rationing problems – and then the trains from London would start arriving with the passengers for the shuttle back – Government diplomats and officials bound for consultations in Washington, American wounded, British military personnel intended for special training, and, most numerous of all, German prisoners of war, three or four thousand of them at a time, heading for Canadian camps or the cotton fields of Alabama as twentieth-century slave labour.

It was the enemy who, for the journey back to New York, or sometimes to Halifax, Nova Scotia, kept the standee bunks warm for the next load of G.I.s. And they proved trouble-free passengers – so trouble-free, in fact, that when Winston Churchill wanted to cross the Atlantic to see President Roosevelt in May 1943 he went in the *Queen Mary* along with 5,000 German prisoners of war. 'I could not see what harm they could do us under due control and without weapons, so I gave instructions that they should come along.'

It was the first of three voyages that Churchill made in the *Queen Mary* across the wartime Atlantic – his principal impact on the ship being his breach of its strict wartime teetotalism. His one regret that he gave the Queens so unconditionally to the U.S.A. was that American military regulations turned them both into 'dry' ships, and he made sure when he crossed the Atlantic himself that he took his own licensing regulations with him, though he was horrified to discover even then that the Cunard stewards, in an excess of enthusiasm for wartime austerity, poured out glasses of water before uncorking the champagne – a style of thrift he very quickly put an end to.

The Prime Minister's quarters were completely sealed off from the rest of the ship and were not only restored to pre-war comfort but also converted into a suite of offices and guard rooms which became for the duration of the voyage the floating headquarters of Britain's war effort. Chiefs of Staff and military experts, Cabinet Ministers, cipher clerks, spy ring operators, detectives, bodyguards and Churchill's secretaries, including his daughter Mary, all had their own offices and state-rooms in the ship – a moving microcosm of Whitehall. Thus it was while lying in bed in his chintz state-room on the *Queen Mary*'s M Deck, that the Prime Minister had explained to him for the first time all the details of 'Overlord', the Allied invasion of Europe projected for the following year.

Above the G.I. queues, the map with working models that each liner used to show the positions of the Queens as they crossed the North Atlantic

American bomber squadron crew entertain themselves during the long gap between the two set meals of the day. Note the metal standee bunks

This was on Churchill's second wartime voyage in August 1943. On the first, a few months previously, there had been a plague of bed bugs which left the Prime Minister unscathed, but which were less than kind to Lady Beveridge, on a working honeymoon with her husband. Beveridge had government business to discuss with Churchill and thus had to endure with his bride honeymoon breakfasts in the company of one of Britain's more sardonic Prime Ministers. 'What's the matter, Beveridge?' enquired the tyrant one morning, noticing how the lady had been bitten and the husband spared. 'Are you sleeping apart?'

Churchill enjoyed himself thoroughly on his three ocean voyages across the wartime Atlantic. Lord Alanbrooke came on one of them, Guy Gibson, fresh from leading the Dam Busters raid on another, and with him was Brigadier Wingate, discussing with Churchill his strategy for the brilliant Chindit campaigns in Burma. It made the *Queen Mary* even more of an attraction for a U-boat commander – the principal Allied target on land or sea, in fact, but though Hitler offered £100,000 to the ship that could sink one of the Queens, the Germans could never get near either of them.

'Built for the arts of peace and to link the Old World with the New,' said Churchill, 'the Queens challenged the fury of Hitlerism in the Battle of the Atlantic. At a speed never before realized in War, they carried over a million men to defend the liberties of civilization.

'Often whole divisions at a time were moved by each ship. Vital decisions depended upon their ability continuously to elude the enemy, and without their aid the day of final victory must unquestionably have been postponed. To the men who contributed to the success of our operations in the years of peril, and to those who brought these two great ships into existence, the world owes a debt that it will not be easy to measure.'

As the troops who had crossed the Atlantic in the dark and dangerous days streamed homeward triumphant on the same great liners that had taken them to Europe, Winston Churchill, also resting from his labours, sailed with them in the *Queen Elizabeth* on 9 January 1946. And on the day before they reached New York, the 12,314 soldiers on board broke off from their standee swapping and mess queue shifts to cheer a speech delivered to them by the ex-Prime Minister:

'My friends and shipmates in the *Queen Elizabeth*. For most of you it is homeward-bound . . .

'The seas are clear, the old flag flies and those who have done the work turn home again, their task accomplished, their duty done.

'What a strange, fearful yet glittering chapter this war has been!

'What changes it has wrought throughout the world, and in the fortunes of so many families! What an interruption in all the plans each of us had made! What a surrender of the liberties we prized! What a casting away of comfort and safety! What a pride in peril! What a glory shines on the brave and the true!

'The good cause has not been overthrown. Tyrants have been hurled from their place of power, and those who sought to enslave the future of mankind have paid, or will pay, the final penalty . . .

'Yesterday I was on the bridge, watching the mountainous waves and this ship, which is no pup, cutting through them and mocking their anger. I asked myself, why is it that the ship beats the waves, when they are so many and the ship is one?

'The reason is that the ship has a purpose and the waves have none. They just flop around, innumerable, tireless, but ineffective. The ship with the purpose takes us where we want to go. Let us therefore have purpose both in our national and imperial policy, and in our own private lives. Thus the future will be fruitful for each and for all, and the reward of the warriors will not be unworthy of the deeds they have done!'

9. THE RAMMING OF H.M.S. CURACOA

The cruiser H.M.S. *Curacoa* – it was cut in half by the *Queen Mary* in 1942. The *Curacoa* went to the bottom with the loss of 338 lives. In the engine room of the *Queen Mary* a small jolt was felt. The damage to the liner's bows (top left) did not stop her sailing to the Clyde and then back to America before being repaired

On 18 May 1945 the Lords of the Admiralty published the list of ships that had been lost during the course of hostilities on the North Atlantic and among them was H.M.S. *Curacoa*, 4,200 tons, 456 feet long, and armed with eight 4-inch guns, a cruiser that had been commissioned to escort the *Queen Mary* in the autumn of 1942. Her loss had been one of the better kept secrets of the war, for she had been sunk, with the loss of 338 men, by the *Queen Mary* herself.

It had happened after lunch on 2 October 1942 as the *Queen Mary*, with 10,000 G.I.s aboard, zig-zagged round the north of Ireland through the U-boat ridden water off Bloody Foreland and Arran Island. She was nearly home and had been joined at nine o'clock that morning by the anti-submarine escort which consisted of six destroyers and one anti-aircraft cruiser steaming close to starboard – the *Curacoa*.

The standard and agreed procedure as look-outs of the naval escort scanned the sea and sky for enemy mines and raiders was for the *Queen Mary* to continue the great zig-zags with which she and her sister ship traversed the Atlantic. The zig-zags added some forty-eight hours to each of the liners' crossing times, but they made torpedo attack almost impossible. At unpredictable intervals the liner would change course in an unpredictable direction which meant it was impossible for a U-boat commander to anticipate a line into which he could aim his torpedoes. On board the Queen the Cunard navigator knew exactly what he was doing, but the whole object of the exercise was to confuse any other vessel trying to chart his tack. And though it was in theory possible to tell escorting warships which way the liner was about to veer, in practice the Royal Navy adopted a rule of thumb that simply involved keeping well out of the big ship's way.

For reasons never satisfactorily explained, H.M.S. *Curacoa* on that rough but clear October afternoon in 1942 broke the rule. And, indeed, when Navigating Officer Stanley Wright on the pill-boxed and sand-bagged bridge of the *Queen Mary* noticed that the *Curacoa* was getting dangerously close, he asked the master, Captain Cyril Illingworth, whether he should take avoiding action, only to be told:

'You need not worry about the cruiser. These fellows know all about escorting; he will keep out of your way.'

And Captain Illingworth was, in theory, quite correct. The *Curacoa* had escorted the *Queen Mary* through these waters three times before and her master, Captain John Boutwood, D.S.O., knew the drill.

Captain Boutwood was, in fact, the senior officer in command of the entire escort force and he had sent his six destroyers on ahead to sweep the waters through which the *Queen Mary* would pass. His plan was to station himself just behind his charge, acting as anti-aircraft protection while the ships ahead kept a look-out for mines and submarines. On an open ocean, on a clear day, it seemed as unimaginable to the participants in the tragedy as it does to us now that two ships with the whole of the Atlantic to choose from should select courses that made for collision – and should not take evasive action when they realized the danger. Both were quite confident, until too late, that the other would get out of the way.

At ten past two Senior First Officer Noel Robinson, on the bridge of the *Queen Mary*, finally wondering whether the cruiser he could see so clearly and so close was not, perhaps, quite aware of the converging course she was steering, ordered the liner's helmsman to veer away from her to port a little. And at almost the same moment Captain Boutwood on the bridge of the *Curacoa* ordered his own helmsman to steer off in the opposite direction.

'Starboard 15. Just to be on the safe side.'

But the safe side was not enough. Both ships were moving fast and their casual veerings without any reduction of speed made little immediate difference to their collision course. In the heavy swell both were yawing in a fashion that carried each several degrees out of true. And once they were really close, forces of interaction set up by their respective bow waves and washes made avoiding action impossible. They were drawn towards each other remorselessly.

Down in the *Queen Mary*'s engine rooms the engineers felt a slight bump and thought the liner had hit a large wave. Captain Illingworth in the chart room, calculating for the benefit of the *Curacoa* his estimated time of arrival in the Clyde, also felt it and wondered whether the liner had been caught by a German bomber as he had often feared it might. But the *Queen Mary* kept steaming ahead powerfully. Whatever had caused the knock had obviously left the liner unharmed.

Captain Boutwood and the *Curacoa*, however, knew all about the bump, for the *Queen Mary* had struck the stern of the cruiser a glancing blow, wheeled the whole ship bodily round so she lay right across the front of the liner's great bows and then cut straight through her like a cleaver through mincemeat. As the *Queen Mary* ploughed on without pause towards the horizon, the two halves of the *Curacoa* drifted in separate directions in her wash to sink within minutes beneath the icy waves of the Atlantic. Of the 439 officers and ratings on board the *Curacoa*, 338 lost their lives, drowned, mashed into pieces by the liner's propellers or crushed by the great steel bows ploughing through their quarters to slice the warship in two. Captain Boutwood was one of the 101 survivors picked up by the destroyers who turned back as soon as they heard of the disaster, the *Queen Mary* herself steaming steadily on towards her destination as her wartime orders strictly enjoined her to. She must never stop or turn round, whatever the circumstances.

In the Clyde it was discovered that her stern had been buckled back so as to staunch dangerous leakages and that she was sufficiently unaffected to sail back across the Atlantic for repairs. But Lord Haw-Haw got the news and was happy to broadcast it, while after the war there was a prolonged legal postmortem to determine who should pay compensation to the relatives of the 338 dead. If the *Curacoa* had been negligent, then normal Admiralty rules of sea service applied: a pension plus, possibly, a little extra compensation. But if the *Queen Mary* were to blame then Cunard, who had been operating the ship on behalf of the American government, could be sued for substantial damages.

The action was a long one involving Trinity House masters sitting as advisers to Mr Justice Pilcher. Scale-model tests were carefully staged and observed in the water tanks of the National Physical Laboratory at Teddington – and judgement went to Cunard. The *Curacoa* was found to be negligent and totally responsible for the collision. But the Lords of the Admiralty appealed and secured the judgement that the cruiser was only two-thirds to blame. The *Queen Mary*, decided the appeal judges, *did* have some degree of responsibility for the disaster – $33\frac{1}{3}$ per cent responsibility to be precise – and this was an allocation which the House of Lords upheld when Cunard appealed.

So after two further legal actions – test cases for a married man and for a bachelor to determine the exact level at which damages should be set – it was nearly a decade before Cunard had to pay out compensation for the accident. And by the time the sad affair of H.M.S. *Curacoa* was finally concluded, the Queens of the North Atlantic were enjoying happier days.

10. THE G.I. BRIDES

1,200 G.I. brides and their babies were
carried by the *Queen Mary* in the spring
and summer of 1946. This photograph was
taken on the promenade deck in mid-Atlantic

War had ended, but there was one last mission to accomplish before the two Queens could both be demobilized. There were some 25,000 European girls – most of them British – who had married the American servicemen that the Queens had ferried across the ocean during the years of war. And now these G.I. brides – together with some 15,000 newborn children – needed to be carried across the North Atlantic to their new homes.

With hostilities concluded, the new peace-time leaders of the Anglo-American alliance, Attlee and Truman, enjoyed a somewhat less generous relationship than had flourished between their predecessors, Churchill and Roosevelt, and, keen to redeem his pledges to the troops who had voted him into power, Attlee was particularly anxious to get the far-flung British army home and de-mobbed. So less than a week after Japan had been bombed into capitulation, Attlee cabled Truman demanding the immediate return of the Queens and the *Aquitania*, and after some haggling the compromise reached was that Britain should have back the oldest and newest of the trio immediately, but that the *Queen Mary* would carry out her special assignment with the G.I. brides.

So while the *Aquitania* and *Queen Elizabeth* came back to Southampton to be refitted for peace-time passenger service – the former after over thirty years that had seen two world wars, the latter in preparation for the mufti maiden voyage that she had still to make – the *Queen Mary*, between February and May 1946 transported across the North Atlantic 12,886 new Americans – 3,768 of them being children. Out came the standee bunks and in their place were built cots and nappy rooms and nurseries, while the ladies who were the living testimony to the success of the Queens' 'Getting-to-know-Europe' classes were themselves daily presented with a freshly devised course of instruction – on life in the States.

The *Queen Mary*'s arrival in New York had always been a spectacular occasion, but the receptions she got as she brought her cargoes of brides and children into the harbour in 1946 were unprecedented. All the spouting fire tenders came out in force together with hooting tugs and aeroplanes circling overhead. Anticipating a certain amount of confusion, the reception authorities had worked out a system of wired enclosures into which the brides were herded according to the state for which they were bound; then their husbands were summoned for reunions in alphabetical order. But Smiths and Zubinskys are men as passionate as Abrahams and Browns and, driven by the pangs of separation, would slide down pillars, jump ropes, break down doors, do anything, in fact, to embrace their beloveds without alphabetical delay. And so the Cunard reception pier in the spring of 1946 became the scene of the wildest scrimmages, children screaming and women crying as men fought their way past barriers and officials to their spouses – while mothers-in-law looked down disapprovingly from the galleries above.

Samuel Cunard would have been pleased that scenes of similar emotion – though in more restrained Canadian fashion – were repeated in Nova Scotia later that summer as the *Queen Mary*, having ferried her last cargo of G.I. brides, brought into Halifax a series of loads of new Canadian wives and children. Then, at long last, on 29 September 1946, after over a year working for military authorities in time of peace, the *Queen Mary* returned to Southampton finally to be de-mobbed.

Opposite: stepping into a new life – G.I. brides bound for New York in the summer of '46

11. DEMOBILISATION

The *Queen Mary* returns from war service
in camouflage paint. In the background, the
Queen Elizabeth, refurbished in
her Cunard livery, awaits her civilian
maiden voyage

The reconditioning of the Queens so that they could at last begin the two-way greyhound service for which they had been conceived over twenty years earlier provoked not a little controversy in post-war Britain. The Government decided that the *Queen Elizabeth* should be refurbished in all her glory as proof to the world that 'Britain can make it'. But Britons deprived of housing and rationed to the last lump of sugar resented the special exceptions made for the sake of a gin palace decked out to catch the fancy of film stars and dollar millionaires. So the Cunard publicity machine went into action to point out that most of their fittings and furniture had been prepared and set aside before the war, republishing the list of materials given in a *Times* report of 1938 'to show that the ship has not been completed at the expense of the present needs of British homes.'

There were ghosts in the grand saloons of the great liners – the vanished hopes and pleasures of the 1930s and, more tangibly, the lingering presence of one and a half million servicemen, a Grand Army of Kilroys who had marked their passage with an all-enveloping cobweb of scribblings and carvings. There was one school of thought in favour of retaining the wooden deck-rails of the Queens scarred with the initials of regiments, loved ones, and comrades, and so, for a time, they escaped the joiner's plane. But Cunard was never a company noted for sentimentality – or a sense of history – and perhaps in 1946 they were right. For their two great liners, now the make-or-break factors in the company's economic survival, were already dangerously close to being historical monuments themselves. People were anxious to forget the war, and so the two Queens were refurbished in a fashion that entered into that conspiracy.

While the *Queen Mary* kept up her trooping with the G.I. brides, layers of camouflage were chipped off the *Queen Elizabeth* to be replaced, for the first time, by thirty tons of paint in the company colours. Her twenty-six motor lifeboats took on at last the sparkling white liveries to which they were entitled. One hundred and twenty lady french polishers worked feverishly at the special skills of their craft. 4,500 settees, chairs and tables, 4,000 mattresses, 6,000 curtains and bedspreads, 2,000 carpets and 1,500 wardrobes and dressing-tables, were taken out of moth balls. And finally, in the autumn of 1946, the *Queen Elizabeth* was ready properly to enjoy all the ballyhoo that had marked her sister's maiden voyage ten years earlier and which she had had to forgo in 1940.

The appropriate royal parties turned up, a good deal older and more serious now. The little princesses had grown out of Mickey Mouse films and wielded stopwatches instead of dolls. They gravely measured the liner's time over a test mile – 2 minutes 1·3 seconds – and a couple of special trains carried members of both Houses of Parliament down to inspect the great liner in which they felt they had an interest – though Cunard had paid off the last of their debts to the government back in 1941.

Newspapers made their readers' mouths water with the menu served to the lucky passengers on the maiden voyage.

Grapefruit au Kirsch.

Hors d'Oeuvres Variés.

Soup: – Consommé Royal, Cream of Mushroom.

Fish: – Red Mullet Meunière, Halibut, Sauce Mousseline.

Entrées: – Croquette of Duckling, Tête de Veau Vinaigrette.

Joint: – Leg and Shoulder of Lamb with Mint Sauce.

Vegetables: – Green Peas, Cauliflower.

Potatoes: – Boiled, Roast, Snow and Gaufrette.
Relève: – Roast Turkey, Chipolata Sauce.
Salad: – Salade Cressonière.
Grill: – Devilled Ham and Succotash.
Sweets: – Orange soufflé Pudding; Coupe Monte Carlo, Macedoine of Fruit Chantilly.
Ices: – Vanilla, Strawberry, Lemon with Petit Fours.
There are also fresh fruit and coffee, of course.

Then the reports added primly, to forestall letters of protest from the ration-book burdened multitudes, that all these delicacies had been purchased in the United States and Canada and brought over the Atlantic on the *Aquitania*. Britain's contribution to the Cunard cornucopia had been just the potatoes and the boiling fish – which of course, was just about the fare the average British newspaper reader was enjoying in 1946.

Panic was caused on the Stock Exchange when Sir Hugo Cunliffe-Owen, the tobacco baron, collapsed as the liner left Southampton, but his company share price recovered once it was learned what his trouble had been – over-eating. And the ship's surgeon was kept busy all the way to New York coping with digestive systems over-strained after years of wartime abstinence. Even King George VI himself when first he visited the ship was seen to have borne away for his breakfast next morning white rolls in not-so-discreet paper bags, for white flour was hard to come by in the late 1940s, in Buckingham Palace as elsewhere.

Nor was it only the bloated rich who revelled in this sudden orgy of plenty. Comrades Molotov and Vishinsky sailed on the maiden voyage of the *Queen Elizabeth* bound for the first session of the United Nations in New York. Mr Molotov was even feeling playful enough to be photographed at the wheel of the great liner and steered, it was subsequently reported, somewhat to the left.

The one shadow over the carnival lights was the sudden death just before the liner sailed of the man who was to preside over all the festivities – Sir Percy Bates. He was the man who, truly, had made it all possible and, in mid-Atlantic, a memorial service recorded his passing in appropriate fashion. The liner's dance band played his favourite hymn, 'Praise, my Soul, the King of Heaven'.

Meanwhile, back in Southampton, the Clydesiders who had been brought down to a special work-camp to renovate the *Queen Elizabeth* had already started work on the *Queen Mary*. Miss Doris Zinkeisen was commissioned to execute two more murals in her own inimitable style – 'The Chase' and 'Hunting Through the Ages', 'gay, vivid compositions, with mermaids in scarlet jackets and underwater revelry in the realm of Neptune.' The starboard gallery and ballroom were turned into a cinema – films had previously been screened in the darkened lounge – with a decor all of plastic. While, a sign of the times, some of the crew were provided with more civilized accommodation. The old gymnasium was converted into a wardroom for the engineers.

On 25 July 1947, as she was returning from her first 'shake down' cruise in the Channel, the *Queen Mary* met for the first time in peacetime colours the *Queen Elizabeth* sailing round the Isle of Wight for New York, and less than a week later, on 31 July 1947, she sailed from Southampton on her first civilian post-war voyage. The next day, on 1 August, her sister ship set sail in the opposite direction from New York. Cunard's two-ship weekly shuttle service across the North Atlantic had finally begun.

12. THE QUEENS OF THE NORTH ATLANTIC

The passenger lists of the Queens were a *Who's Who* of the '40s and '50s. From left to right (top row): Mr and Mrs David Niven, Rita Hayworth, Burt Lancaster and entourage; (centre row) Spencer Tracy, Alan Ladd, Randolph Turpin and trainers; (bottom row) the Windsors and Bing Crosby

For twenty years the two Queens straddled the North Atlantic and made it their own. Bigger and faster ships were built – the *France* was longer than either Queen, the *United States*, built under military contract, phenomenally faster than any liner the world has ever seen – but none could supplant the twin Cunarders in the affections of transatlantic passengers. And when the Queens got stabilizers in the mid-1950s they even became comfortable to travel in.

Their appeal lay in their style or rather their lack of it – a chintzy, typically British compromise between the snob and the crass that contrived to charm in circumstances where others would infuriate. Cunard captains and commodores sporting the knighthoods that were, for a period, lavished upon the mariners of Britain's premier steamship line, set the tone that was always derived from the example set by the legendary master of the *Aquitania*, Commodore Sir James Charles, a gentleman whose tastes at table were, said Lucius Beebe:

> . . . vaguely those of Emil Jannings playing Henry VIII. Stewards wheeled in carcasses of whole roasted oxen one night and the next evening small herds of grilled antelope surrounded a hilltop of Strasbourg *foie gras* surmounted with peacock fans. Electrically illuminated *pièces montées* representing the Battle of Waterloo and other patriotic moments made an appearance while the ship's orchestra played Elgar. Chefs in two-foot high hats emerged to make thrusts in tierce at turrets of Black Angus that towered above the arched eyebrows of the diners, and soufflés the size of the chefs' hats blossomed towards the end, like the final set pieces of a Paine's fireworks display on the Fourth of July. Through these flanking movements and skirmishes champagne circulated in jeroboams – Mumm's 1916, Irroy, and Perrier Jouet, ditto.
>
> Sir James Charles, a grandee of the sea lanes so portly and full of honours that his mess jackets required structural bracing in their internal economy to support the weight of his decorations, died in line of duty, at sea, almost literally leading an assault on a citadel of pastry moated with diamond back turtle stew *au Madeira*. When they took him ashore at Southampton it was necessary to open both wings of the *Aquitania*'s half-ports to accommodate his going. It was the exit of a nobleman and a warrior.

Sir James's successors never quite summoned up the *braggadocio* to match his achievement but, 'yokels in uniform' though they might be, they managed to trick out their basic seaman's habits with sufficient social swank to be taken by most of their passengers for aristocracy, if not royalty. Ladies dressed up and curtsied for them. Businessmen who could buy the whole ship several times over were anxious for invitations to their cocktail parties, while titled persons seemed to prize a seat at the captain's table as highly as a dinner party at the Palace.

Right to the end of the swinging sixties social etiquette was strictly preserved on the Queens – in First Class at least. On the first and last nights of the voyage gentlemen wore dark business suits to dinner while ladies wore party outfits. On the intervening evenings it was black ties and evening gowns. Every evening at a quarter past seven the select fifteen summoned by the Captain's engraved invitation card would gather in his cabin for cocktails. Then, an hour later, the party would move down to the dining room, the guests fanning out to their tables, the Captain striding on through the passengers greeting those he did – and did not – know, finally to arrive at his own round table where seven super-selected passengers awaited him. The cocktail fifteen changed personnel every evening. But the Captain's Table seven retained their places throughout the voyage.

How did he make his selections, this simple salt who had to keep in his head not only the manuals of navigation and seamanship but *Who's Who*, *Debrett*, and

Cabin steward on the *Queen Elizabeth*. Following pages: a small portion of the *Queen Elizabeth*'s 55,000 pieces of silver and silver plate

the *Almanach de Gotha* as well? It was not all his own work. Cunard had little staffs of specialists both in London and New York, well versed in the gradations of significance to be accorded passengers on account of their title, wealth or connections. 'Although the Company never exert any pressure as to who is to sit where,' explained one Captain, 'there is naturally a tendency to consider its commercial interests where influential passengers are concerned.'

There were some passengers who could phone up Cunard and obtain a voyage-long reservation in the Verandah Grill only a day before they sailed, while others could try to book months ahead to be told, mysteriously and with great regret that there just wasn't a spare inch of space for even one meal at any time during their trip. With such undemocratic little discriminations did the Queens guard their cachet. Cunarder life was governed by the rules of a discreet, dinner-jacketed jungle, the Captain only intervening to embargo Lord so-and-so's less than honest pontoon school or cut off the liquor supplies to such-and-such an oil millionaire's table when they had broken the cardinal rule that 'Passengers must not be antagonized unless they antagonize others more valuable to the company than themselves.' So a drunken lord firing off champagne corks could be tolerated – until he hit a wealthy dowager duchess in the eye. An impoverished lady aristocrat would probably have had to grin and bear it.

It was scarcely fair to all, and it was certainly not pleasant for some, but it was the fashion in which the English upper classes had regulated precedence for centuries, and the Queens gave the untitled a chance to play the same game.

Occasionally the system broke down, as when in 1947 the *Queen Elizabeth* ran on to a mudflat in Southampton Water and the Captain only let a chosen few in on the secret. For twenty-six hours the rest of the passengers had to rely 'upon the casual gossip of stewards and deck hands rather than authoritative pronouncements from the bridge', as one letter writer to *The Times* complained. All telegrams leaving the ship were censored in a futile attempt to prevent the news of the grounding getting out ('stuck' was changed to 'delayed'). But the Captain's mistake was to confide in the wrong people. Enraged at being excluded from the charmed circle, Randolph Churchill blew the whole story in the *Daily Telegraph*.

Everyone, however, could enjoy the famous Cunard food at whatever table they sat. Shopping in New York, Southampton, and Cherbourg the Queens' catering superintendents could buy the very best food at the very keenest prices – strawberries flown from California, watermelons trucked from Florida, lobsters from Maine, snails, caviar, grouse – the lists become more and more exotic through the fifties and sixties as the liners competed with the aeroplanes flying ever more numerous and rapidly overhead. The provisions list for an average summer voyage made incredible reading:

Biscuits	1,100 lb.	Dried fruits	1,300 lb.
Cereals (breakfast)	500 lb.	Fish (canned)	1,150 lb.
Cereals (breakfast packets)	1,000 lb.	Fruit (canned) No. 10 size	1,350 cans
Cereals	800 lb.	Fruit (canned) No. 2½ size	1,300 cans
Flour of all kinds	20,000 lb.	Mustards (various)	
Macaroni, spaghetti,		peppers, spices, and herbs	150 lb.
noodles	550 lb.	Salt	2,400 lb.
Oatmeal and rolled oats	450 lb.	Conserves, fruit	45 lb.

Honey and Ginger, preserved	35 lb.	Blueberries	100 lb.
Jams and Marmalade	1,050 jars	Grapes (choice)	1,500 lb.
Jams and Marmalade 7 lb.	75 cans	Grapefruit	90 boxes
Jellies (various)	115 lb.	Lemons	35 boxes
Syrups (various)	30 gall.	Limes	1,000
Juices, fruit, and vegetable No. 10	850 cans	Melons (various)	2,800
		Nectarines	300
Juices, fruit, and vegetable No. 5	1,900 cans	Oranges (various)	18,000
Nuts (various)	550 lb.	Tangerines	100 lb.
Pickles and Olives	800 bottles	Peaches	500
Sauces, ketchups, and chutneys	900 bottles	Pears (various)	1,150 lb.
		Strawberries and other soft fruits in season	2,250 lb.
Salad oil	160 gall.	Pineapples	75
Turtle soups etc.	475 pints	Fresh frozen fruits	1,500 lb.
Cup chocolate and cocoa	41 lb.	Ice cream	4,000 qts.
Coffee (various brands)	1,700 lb.	Choice loins, beef	19,000 lb.
Sugar (cube, granulated, etc.)	7,500 lb.	Choice rib beef	1,250 lb.
		Choice fillets beef	1,150 lb.
Teas (various)	1,100 lb.	Beef (various)	2,000 lb.
Vinegars	200 pints	Beef (corned)	1,500 lb.
Vegetables (canned and purée)	3,500 cans	Lamb (including joints)	10,100 lb.
		Pork (including joints)	2,500 lb.
Strained foods, infants	300 cans	Pork (corned)	850 lb.
Essences	25 bottles	Veal	1,850 lb.
Bacon	5,150 lb.	Offals (various)	3,650 lb.
Hams	2,500 lb.	Tongues (corned and smoked)	1,250 lb.
Cheeses	1,800 lb.		
Butter	5,900 lb.	Chickens (broiling)	1,900 lb.
Eggs	70,250	Chickens (squab)	175 lb.
Cream	3,250 qts.	Chickens (Guinea)	115 lb.
Milk (fresh)	24,250 pints	Chickens (Roasting)	6,500 lb.
Milk (evaporated)	600 gall.	Chickens (Poussin)	90 lb.
Margarine and lard	2,250 lb.	Poulardes de Bress	900 lb.
Fish (fresh and shell)	19,500 lb.	Poulets de Grain	600 lb.
Fish (smoked)	1,450 lb.	Pigeons (various)	425 lb.
Salmon (smoked)	425 lb.	Turkeys (Tom)	5,050 lb.
Sturgeon (smoked)	50 lb.	Turkeys (Hen)	225 lb.
Snails	300	Turkeys (Smoked)	50 lb.
Scallops and clams	125 gall.	Sausages (Breakfast, etc.)	2,150 lb.
Apples (40 lb. boxes)	300 boxes	Vegetables	41,000 lb.
Apricots (dessert)	100 lb.	Vegetables (Frozen)	8,750 lb.
Bananas	1,450 lb.	Potatoes	55,000 lb.

Queen Elizabeth, July 1948. American shuffleboard devotee: he refused to reveal his name when approached by the cameraman

New-look businessman – bound for Europe. In the late '40s and '50s Cunard carried 30 per cent of all Atlantic passenger traffic, earning, on average, £7 million a year

Afternoon tea on first-class promenade deck. In the lounge the string orchestra presented Music for Tea Time. In the smoke room there was bridge

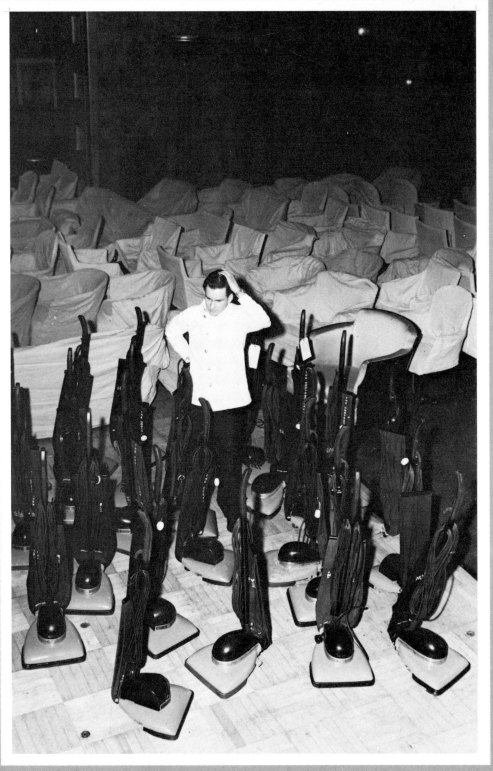

Annual overhaul for the *Queen Elizabeth*, 1953. A trainee steward checks a bewildering
array of vacuum cleaners

Kosher diets were provided for with 200 pounds of beef ribs, 24 cartons of matzoh, 24 drums of heimische cucumber, 60 pounds of Kosher cheese, gefüllte fish, Kosher ice cream, margarine and cooking oil, and 100 chicken and 100 ducks slaughtered under the supervision of the Beth Din.

The wine, spirit, and tobacco list was equally gargantuan, and its stupendous potential for inspiring merriment in its consumers makes it somewhat more appealing than the ultimately sickening catalogue of foodstuffs loaded for each voyage:

	Bottles	½ Bottles			
Champagne	2,400	1,440	Cognac (3 star)	300	–
French Sparkling Burgundy	300	180	Armagnac	24	–
			Rum	360	–
Red Bordeaux	960	720	Scotch Whisky	2,400	–
White Bordeaux	720	480	Irish Whisky	120	–
Red Burgundy	600	600	American Whisky	1,200	–
White Burgundy	420	300	Canadian Whisky	480	–
Rhone	60	72	Gin	1,200	–
Rhone Rosé	240	–	Aperitifs, Vermouth, etc.	2,504	–
Alsatian	60	–			
Rhine	600	480	Ale and beer	6,000	–
Moselle	300	288	Stout	2,400	–
Rhine and Moselle Sparkling	180	–	Lager	12,000	–
			Lager (draught)	6,000 gall.	–
Chianti	–	132			
American Wines	36	–	American beer and ale	2,400	–
Empire Wines	192	–	Cider	240	–
Port	168	–	Mineral waters	48,000	–
Sherry	480	–	Cordials	360	–
Cooking wines	144	–	Cigarettes (no.)	1,500,000	
Liqueurs	672	–	Tobacco	240 (lb.)	
Cognac, Fine Champagne, etc.	180	–	Cigars (no.)	15,000	

Attention to detail made the Queens what they were. At dawn every morning the ship's gardener got up for his daily watering can patrol of the twelve thousand plants each liner carried on every voyage: begonias, hydrangeas, fuchsias, lilies and ferns, he grew them all, and in glass-fronted refrigerators on the sun deck kept cut flowers for special bouquets and buttonholes – orchids, carnations, rosebuds. One of his duties was to make up mid-ocean bouquets ordered by telegram from either shore – and to care for the flowers of the famous. One gardener catalogued his clients' attitudes to floral decoration. Elizabeth the Queen Mother, he said, 'loves them'; Sir Winston Churchill 'never takes the slightest notice of them, though Lady Churchill does'; when the Duke of Windsor travelled on the liner he had inspected as King, the Duchess would, apparently, always bring her own vases; and Lord Beaverbrook 'always insists on having flowers in his state-

Following pages: in 1948 ships' bellboys started at the age of 15 and could earn up to £10 per month

room when he comes on board, then rings the bell and says "get those damned things out of here".'

That was not the only eccentricity of the great press baron for, like many English passengers, he was annoyed by the staging calls the Queens always made at Cherbourg. It was not far out of the way in terms of distance, but in terms of time all the anchoring, unloading, and re-embarking of cargo and passengers in the French port added half a day to the voyage. On the way out it increased the fun. On the way home it was just tedious, so Lord Beaverbrook would get into an aeroplane at Cherbourg and fly home across the channel.

Cunard did, in fact, consider, having special catapult planes fitted to each of the Queens for passengers who were keen to save time at the end of the journey – and who were prepared to pay for the time that this saved. In the 1920s and 1930s both the *Île de France* and the *Bremen* had carried such catapult planes which, twenty-four hours away from their liner's destination, would blast off bearing special 'air' mails and, occasionally, passengers in a hurry. The torpedo like take-offs to the cheers of the entire ship's company proved most successful social occasions, but by the time Cunard got round to considering the notion, shore-to-shore airliners had made catapult take-offs irrelevant.

There was, besides, more than enough to occupy a passenger on a Cunarder Queen in the forties, fifties, and early sixties. Each day began with a discreet knock on the cabin door and the appearance of your steward – or stewardess – bearing a steaming pot of tea on a tray. Both liners had been designed so that passengers could, if they wished, bring their own retainers – and even, in some state-rooms, have their meals cooked and served privately. But even if you lacked your own private Jeeves, breakfast in the dining room was not too ignoble an affair: a choice of eighty different dishes, eleven types of cereal, tea from Ceylon, India, or China, and five different sorts of toast. Then you could read your *Ocean Times*, the liner's very own newspaper printed on the ship's presses during the night and retailing a strange combination of world news and the latest positions in the Main Deck Shuffleboard League; or you could get down to Shuffleboard your-self, if you were not feeling energetic enough for a swim in the pool. Sporting types who preferred their excitement to be 100 per cent vicarious could limit their exercise to a stroll to the purser's office and the purchase of a sweepstake ticket.

To shake down your five-course lunch you could do worse than put yourself in the muscular hands of the gym instructor or his fast-vibrating machine, the Camel. The Archbishop of Canterbury tried this in 1953, coming back from America in order to officiate at the coronation, and fell heavily on his head. Don Valenti, the *Queen Mary*'s former boxer turned gym coach, couldn't sleep for the rest of the voyage worrying whether Princess Elizabeth would get crowned properly.

There was the Turkish bath, the cinema, the daily symphony concert on record, the shopping arcade, the chapel or the synagogue, depending on how best you liked to wait for tea. Then, replete with scones and muffins, it was time to dress for dinner. Lady passengers would queue at the purser's office to pick up the jewellery they had left in his safe, and all over the ship a score of cocktail shakers started quivering, for those not invited to the captain's cabin would gather in their own little pre-prandial cliques. There were, after all, over a dozen bars on each liner – plus a couple more for the crew.

After dinner the Verandah Grill became the heart of the ship with dancing till the small hours, while bingo callers and bridge scorers regulated the fun of the

Dogs' promenade on the *Queen Mary*

Fingernail inspection on the *Queen Mary*. Bell boys delivered 'General Knowledge' quiz sheets to state-rooms at 7.30 a.m. to occupy the children of sleepy passengers

Radio and film stars Laurel and Hardy in their state-room. Everyone took ashore a bound passenger list with his own name beside those of the famous

Not all the glamour came from Hollywood. British film stars John Mills (right) and Rex Harrison with Lilli Palmer (second left) provided excitement on one voyage

less frenetically chic. And then old and young, First Class and Tourist, all participated, in personal or social communion, in the final ceremony that closed every day on the North Atlantic, shifting several thousand watch hands to allow for the ever-advancing panorama of the changing time zones.

It was a reassuring unvarying ritual that endeared itself to thousands in an uncomfortably changing world. For the price of a ticket you could recapture a vanishing lifestyle, and through the fifties and sixties, the Queens went on making money in the face of increasing competition from air transport. But other liners succumbed to the challenge. The grand old *Aquitania* went to the breaker's yard – though not without placing on record at least one memory of which any liner could be proud. Back in the 1920s, remembered her master, Captain Thelwell, the liner had been docked in Southampton when there was a knock at the door of his cabin.

It was his master-at-arms to say that a party of visitors was about to come aboard. 'Send them away' said the Captain.

'I'm afraid I can't, Sir' said the master-at-arms, 'it's the Prince of Wales with a party of naval officers, and some ladies as well.'

The Captain dressed and went below.

'I peeped into the garden lounge,' he said. 'A dozen negro musicians were already tuning up. The Prince had borrowed a baton and was flexing himself in readiness to conduct. The tall, immaculate figure of Prince Louis Mountbatten was crouched behind the drums with drum-sticks poised and I recognized the King of Greece and the two Greek Princesses Irene and Xenia, with fur coats thrown over their evening dresses. Yet for all the gaiety, the scene had a pale and ghostly setting. The stage, the ornate, half-lit garden lounge was too vast for a handful of people to fill, and it seemed to me sad that a man who was to be monarch soon should be obliged to go to such lengths to get a little innocent amusement for himself and give a little to his friends.'

By the middle of the 1960s the great lounges and ballrooms of the Queens were to be, even in mid-Atlantic, as empty as the *Aquitania* had been, resting between trips in Southampton over a third of a century earlier. It was possible, wrote John Malcolm Brinnin,

'for a single solitary passenger to turn up for tea in the dim depths of the grand saloon and sit, magnificently alone, while a dozen white jacketed stewards stood about like sentries, alert to his command. As he chose his sandwiches and scones and cakes from portable caddies, as all the pyramidal napkins on all the white tables in the gloaming multiplied his sense of isolation, he might notice that a shadowy figure at the furthest end of the room was seating himself at the Wurlitzer. Then, as the great ship creaked and rolled, the intruder would shiver the air with selections from "Rose Marie" and "The Desert Song". Not even the dining room in *Citizen Kane* was emptier.'

Commodore Geoffrey Thripleton Marr, strangely naked without the knighthood which, in an earlier epoch, would have been his automatic due, used to deliver a rather sad little speech at the beginning of such voyages acknowledging to his guests at the Captain's Reception the changed circumstances of oceanic travel and reminding them of the motto that Cunard had dreamed up for the Queens in the air age. 'Getting there is half the fun.'

The trouble was that this desperately intoned legend was a two-edged sword: four storm-tossed days on the North Atlantic could be a good deal less than half the fun of a few hours watching a movie in the calm of the stratosphere. But no one noticed the double meaning – or if they did, they were too polite to point it out.

13. EBB TIDE

31 October 1967. Ship's company of aircraft-carrier H.M.S. *Hermes* 'cheer ship' as the *Queen Mary* sails down the English Channel for the last time. For her last voyage 1,200 passengers paid from £395 to £3,200 per head (for a double suite) on the 39-day voyage around Cape Horn to Long Beach, California

Cruising might be the answer. Through the summers of the sixties the Queens were comfortably filled with holidaymakers. It was when the winter storms began that the dukes and starlets and dollar millionaires deserted Cunard's two old ladies. The *Queen Mary*, over thirty, was too elderly to go gallivanting round the Caribbean. But the *Queen Elizabeth* might, felt Cunard, be able to capitalize on the reputation and affection which represented such sizeable credits to set against both ships' losses on the winter runs.

So in February 1963 the Cunard pier in New York was flooded with sunglasses, sombreros and widows splashing their insurance nest eggs on a five-day trip to Nassau and back. Four bands serenaded as the *Queen Elizabeth* sailed down the Hudson and then veered off southwards away from her customary swing up towards the north-east. There was dancing from noon until dawn, strolling minstrels, fancy-dress parades, non-stop cabarets, mobile bars and a running buffet on the promenade deck. 'It was,' wrote Neil Potter and Jack Frost, 'as if London's Savoy Hotel had engaged Sir Billy Butlin to run it for five days.'

But neither the purists – nor, certainly, the Cunard Steam Ship Company – could really grumble at £150,000 netted in fares before the transatlantic ferry service started up again in the spring. When the time came to overhaul the *Queen Elizabeth* the following winter a new cocktail bar sprouted along with 'new teenage rooms . . . fitted with juke-box, soft-drink machine and a football machine'. There was life left in the old girl yet. She cruised to Nassau again and then struck out on a big seven-port trip to the Mediterranean: Las Palmas, Athens, Tangier, Naples, Cannes, Gibraltar, Lisbon – anywhere for the sake of the stalwart stockholders of Cunard. Even the old *Queen Mary* did her bit, cruising from Southampton to Las Palmas.

It seemed for a while that salvation did lie in cruising and, with plans under way for a completely new Cunarder, the *Queen Elizabeth II*, £1¼ million was spent on refitting the old *Queen Elizabeth* in 1966 for another ten years' service with this new, lithe young running partner: air-conditioning, private showers and lavatories in every cabin and a brand new lido deck complete with swimming pool – the liner's third. Always the ugly sister, the *Queen Mary* was left to rot and rust un-face-lifted.

But it was not to be. Natural justice in the appropriate guise of an air-travel magnate intervened to ensure that the end, which had to come, should at least be neat and dramatically satisfying. On the premise that if they could not beat the aeroplanes they might as well join them, Cunard had linked up with the British Overseas Airways Corporation and acquired a new Chairman, Sir Basil Smallpeice. He proved as adept as any of his predecessors at the old trick which had always infuriated the rest of the British shipping world – dipping Cunard's hand into the public purse, on this occasion to secure funds for the *QE2*. But when he came to look at the £14·1 million that his seven passenger liners had lost in five years he could come to only one conclusion. North Atlantic sea travel had reached a peak of just under one million passengers in 1957. Since then it had fallen steadily towards half that figure, and with all the airlines ordering Jumbo Jets for their transatlantic schedules there was no reason to believe that the trend would be halted. The Queens, decided Cunard with a lack of sentimentality of which old

Top: final resting place for the *Queen Mary* – Long Beach, California. Centre: £3,200,000 was bid by these Philadelphia businessmen for the *Queen Elizabeth* – but the deal fell through. Bottom: sad finale of the *Queen Elizabeth* – gutted in Hong Kong harbour.

Samuel could only have approved, would both have to be retired – and quickly too. In May 1967 the sisters heard their death sentence.

Without more ado the Cunard sales machine set to work around the world on the great liners' behalf touting for holiday camp operators or scrap metal merchants. And their success surpassed their wildest dreams. The *Queen Mary* was sold to the City of Long Beach, California, for $3,400,000 (£1,436,666) and her sister for double the price – $7,750,000 (£3,250,000).

Cunard were able to retort to the ritual dirges in the British press with the assurance that both old ladies would enjoy long and dignified retirements – though all did not go quite according to plan. After a succession of positively final appearances – most profitable little cruises – the *Queen Mary* was despatched on her last long voyage – passenger carrying and money spinning to the last – all the way round Cape Horn up to Long Beach, California, where thousands of red and white carnations were to be dropped on her from the air.

Nor did the problems end when the *Queen Mary* finally berthed in Long Beach, for her conversion costs rocketed to over £20 million before she was finally ready for her new life as a floating museum, convention centre, restaurant, and hotel.

But now, just like the old days, you have to book six months ahead if you want a banquet in one of the great ship's dining rooms, and the Speciality Restaurants Corporation are not disposed either to favour or discourage reservations in the style of the old Cunard social register. The Queen City Record Company has pressed a new signature tune now that Henry Hall's 'Somewhere at Sea' is inappropriate: it is called 'Hail, The Queen' and the flip side celebrates 'Long Beach Town'. There are daily requests for the right to hold marriage ceremonies on board, plans to stage big championship boxing matches for black tie audiences and TV rights and, in keeping with the pride that all Long Beach feels in the liner that is now their own, the local police chief has ordered his men to stop referring to homosexuals as 'queens'.

The *Queen Elizabeth*'s career as a floating Disneyland, however, had no such happy ending. The American company that put down a deposit on her could not raise the balance of the purchase price agreed and so, for a while, Cunard took her over again, opening her to visitors in Port Everglades, Florida before she was auctioned for a second time. Her new owner Mr C. Y. Tung, an obscure but wealthy Chinese shipping magnate who could buy out several of his more famous European counterparts – 'Onassis may have the First Lady, but C.Y. has the Queen' – sent her with her engines at half strength on a slow trip to China where, in Hong Kong harbour, he lavished almost as much on converting her into an educational cruise ship as Cunard did on first building her. She was rechristened the *Seawise University*, a name not unconnected with Mr Tung's own initials, but, in January 1972, only a few days before she was due to sail out on to the ocean in dazzling white glory, she caught fire. Several conflagrations which, said an official court of enquiry, must have been started deliberately by 'a person or persons unknown' combined into a raging firestorm that completely defeated the sprinkler and fireproof bulkhead system that had withstood so many localized blazes in the ship's history. For a day and a night the firemen of Hong Kong hosed water into her until, her belly bloated, she rolled over on to the harbour bottom, her skeleton half submerged and horribly contorted, to become for the junks and launches of Hong Kong harbour a tourist attraction in a style that neither C. Y. Tung nor anyone who loved her could relish.

It is not the way to leave or remember the Queens of the North Atlantic.

EPILOGUE

by John Malcolm Brinnin

12.10 a.m. 25 September 1967.

The *Queen Elizabeth*, largest ship in the world, twenty-seven years old, is bound westward. At some point in the early morning she will meet and pass the *Queen Mary*, the next largest ship in the world, thirty-one years old, bound east. This will be their final meeting, their last sight of one another ever. For more than two decades they have been the proudest sisters on the ocean, deferential to one another, secure in the knowledge that they are the most celebrated things on water since rafts went floating down the Tigris and Euphrates.

Notices of this encounter have been broadcast and posted throughout the ship. But as usual at this hour most passengers have gone to bed, leaving only a few individuals strolling and dawdling on the Promenade Deck. Most of these have chosen to be alone; and they are a bit sheepish, a bit embarrassed, as though ashamed to be seen in the thrall of sentiment, even by others equally enthralled . . .

Spotted, she grows quickly in size and brightness. In the dim silence of the enclosure there are mutters, the click of binoculars against plate glass, an almost reverential sense of breath withheld. On she comes, the *Mary*, with a swiftness that takes everyone by surprise: together the great ships, more than 160,000 tons of steel, are closing the gap that separates them at a speed of nearly sixty miles an hour. Cutting the water deeply, pushing it aside in great crested arrowheads, they veer towards one another almost as if to embrace, and all the lights blaze out, scattering the dark. The huge funnels glow in their Cunard red, the *basso-profundo* horns belt out a sound that has less the quality of a salute than of one long mortal cry. Standing at attention on the portside wing of his flying bridge, the *Elizabeth*'s captain doffs his hat; on the starboard wing of the *Mary* her captain does the same. As though they had not walked and climbed there but had been somehow instantly transported to the topmost deck, the few passengers who have watched the *Mary* come out of the night now watch her go. All through the episode, mere minutes long, have come giggles and petulant whimpers from sequestered corners of the top deck. Indifferent to the moment, untouched by the claims of history, youngsters not yet born when the two Queens were the newest wonders of the world cling together in adolescent parodies of passion and do not bother even to look up. As the darkness closes over and the long wakes are joined, the sentimentalists stand for a while watching the ocean recover its seamless immensity. Then, one by one, like people dispersing downhill after a burial, they find their way to their cabins and close their doors.

(from *The Sway of the Grand Saloon*
published by Delacorte Press and Macmillan)

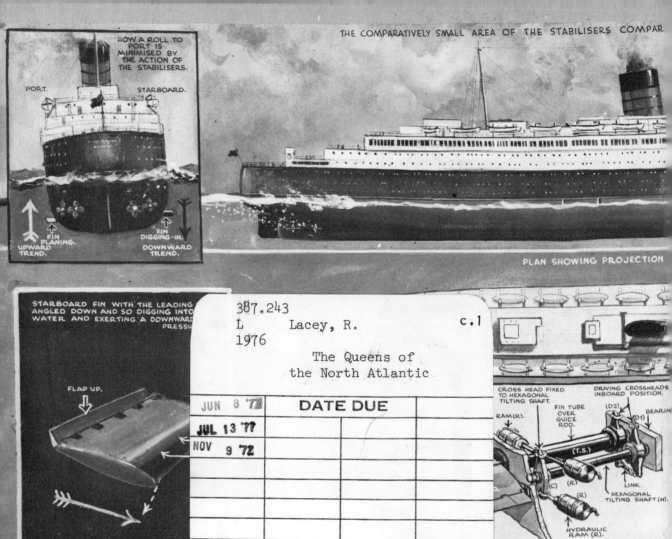

HOW A ROLL TO PORT IS MINIMISED BY THE ACTION OF THE STABILISERS.

PORT. STARBOARD.

FIN PLANING. UPWARD TREND.
FIN DIGGING-IN. DOWNWARD TREND.

THE COMPARATIVELY SMALL AREA OF THE STABILISERS COMPAR...

PLAN SHOWING PROJECTION

STARBOARD FIN WITH THE LEADING... ANGLED DOWN AND SO DIGGING INTO... WATER AND EXERTING A DOWNWARD... PRESSU...

FLAP UP.

CROSS HEAD FIXED TO HEXAGONAL TILTING SHAFT.
DRIVING CROSSHEADS INBOARD POSITION.
(D2)
RAM (R).
FIN TUBE OVER GUIDE ROD.
(D1)
BEARIN...
(T.S.)
(C) (R)
LINK.
HEXAGONAL TILTING SHAFT (H).
(R)
HYDRAULIC RAM (R).

...UBULAR SHAFT (T.S.) WHICH CONTAINS THE HYDR... WHICH ARE CONNECTED TO A CROSS HEAD (C) R... S THE CROSS HEAD (D1) WHICH IS CONNECTED ...EXAGONAL TILTING SHAFT AND THIS IN TURN MOV...

...ATIC VIEW OF THE FORWARD PO...

HOW THE STABILISERS DAMP... THE ROLL OF A SHIP. (COMPARATIVE IMPRESSIONS...

IN AN AVERAGE SEA.

FREE ROLL.
WIT... STABILIS...

IN VERY BAD CONDITION...

FREE ROLL.
WIT... STABILIS...

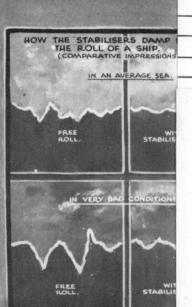

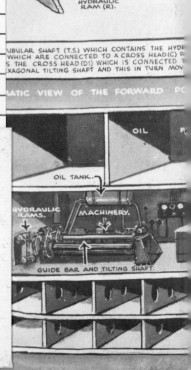

OIL
OIL TANK.
HYDRAULIC RAMS.
MACHINERY.
GUIDE BAR AND TILTING SHAFT.